GO KIDS!

50 FREE and **FUN** things to do **OUTDOORS** with the under 5s in the **BOULDER GOLDEN** area

By Kathryn Pyke

This book belongs to the parents of: . . . .

. . . .

. . . .

. . . .

. . . .

. . . .

. . . .

The author and publisher make no representations or warranties, expressed or implied, of any kind regarding the contents of this book, and expressly disclaim any representation or warranty regarding the accuracy or reliability of information contained herein. There are no warrenties of fitness for a particular purpose or that this book or the information in it are merchantable.

The user assumes all risks associated with the use of this book and with the activities described herein.

PUBLISHED BY:

Wolverine Publishing, 5439 County Rd 243, New Castle, CO 81647, USA.

For more information about Wolverine Publishing, please call 970-984-2815, email dave@wolverinepublishing.com, or visit us on the web at www.wolverinepublishing.com.

© 2006 by Kathryn Pyke
All rights reserved
First edition, 2006
This book or any part thereof may not be reproduced in any form without written permission from the publisher.

INTERNATIONAL STANDARD BOOK NUMBER:

ISBN-10: 0-9721609-8-1
ISBN-13: 978-0-9721609-8-8

LIBRARY OF CONGRESS CATALOG IN PUBLICATION DATA:

Library of Congress Control Number: 2006936440

Printed in China.

Tips: You can buy this book online at: www.wolverinepublishing.com

It is not enough to just 'love nature' or want to 'be in harmony with Gaia'. Our relation to the natural world takes place in a place, and it must be grounded in information and experience.

Gary Snyder

CONTENTS

INTRODUCTION

Why 'play' in nature is good for your child. 12
Finding a special place for nature play. 12
Tips for helping children connect with nature 12
Build on an interest. 14
The Paradox and Leave No Trace ethics. 14
Making a plea to Parks and Recreation Departments. 16
The Future—Green Urban Design. 16
What's Happening Now?. 17

HOW TO USE THIS GUIDE

Purpose of this guide. 18
About the locations. 18
Using the information. 20
Outdoor considerations. 22

BOULDER

1. Ann U. White Trail 24
2. Arapahoe Ridge Park 26
3. Boulder County Recycling Center 28
4. Boulder Creek. 30
5. Chautauqua Park 34
6. Coot Lake/Tom Watson Park. 38
7. Crown Rock. 42
8. CU Campus & Natural History Museum 46
9. East Boulder Community Center 49
10. Eben G. Fine Park 52
11. Eldorado Canyon 55
12. Foothills Community Park 59
13. Goose Creek Greenway. 62
14. Hawthorn Gardens 65
15. Harlow Platts Park 69
16. Lyons 71
17. Marshall Mesa Trail 74
18. Martin Park 76
19. NCAR. 78

BOULDER cont.

20. North Boulder Park 81
21. Pearl Street Mall 84
22. Scott Carpenter Park 87
23. Settlers Park... 89
24. Walden Ponds 91
25. Wonderland Lake.. 93

GOLDEN

1. Arvada Blunn Reservoir... 96
2. Bear Creek Lake Park 99
3. Beverly Heights Park...103
4. Castle Rock...104
5. Clear Creek Sculpture Loop 106
6. Colorado Railroad Museum..109
7. Colorado School Of Mines Geology Trail.................. 111
8. Crown Hill Park.. 113
9. Dinosaur Ridge.. 115
10. Fairmount Park 119
11. Golden Cliffs Preserve 121
12. Golden Gate Canyon State Park 1.............................123
13. Golden Gate Canyon State Park 2 126
14. Jefferson County Fairgrounds...................................129
15. Lions Park and Kayak Park 132
16. Lookout Mountain Nature Center 136
17. North Table Mountain Quarry..................................139
18. Norman D. Memorial Park 141
19. North Golden Bike Loop 143
20. NREL National Renewable Energy Laboratory 146
21. Prospect Park 148
22. Tony Grampsas Memorial Sports Complex..............150
23. Triceratops Trail 152
24. White Ash Mine Park 156
25. White Ranch Park..158

Other Locations: Clear Creek Canyon & I70 Corridor 160
Index...164
References and Further Reading.....................................166
About the Author..168

Ella checking an invasive weed

...there is no science and no art of greater importance than that which teaches seeing, which builds sensitivity and respect for the natural world...
David Brower

DEDICATION
This book is dedicated to Alec and Ella; companions at our local ditch and stream.

In wilderness is the preservation of the world
David Henry Thoreau

I am well again, I came to life in the cool winds and crystal waters of the mountains...
John Muir

INTRODUCTION

> Our children are the first generation to be raised without meaningful contact with the natural world.
>
> *Richard Louv*

When I mention that I'm writing a guide to fun and wild places for the under 5 age group, I always get an enthusiastic "How cool!" and "What fun!" And of course they are right. We live in a state where there's barely a bad weather day, we have an incredible range of geography squeezed onto our foothills doorstep, and as if that was not enough we have a wealth of well cared for parks and open spaces. But something within me does not sit so easily. I also have a more serious issue to broach. Our children are losing touch with nature and its symptoms are pervasive. The phrase 'Nature Deficit Disorder' is increasingly being used to describe the cost to children of not getting enough time in the outdoors. Put simply, they lack the day to day contact with the elements and their heath is suffering; their senses diminished, attention levels reduced and their physical and emotional well being affected*.

That is not to say our children are not aware of the Great Outdoors. Media bombards us with all-action nature and outdoor lifestyle images—a grizzly bear rips apart a writhing salmon, kids raft through raging torrents. But watching such images on TV is a passive experience and bears little resemblance to our everyday lives. We need to be 'tuned-in' to more 'intimate drama'—the reality of an ant struggling to bring a half dead insect into its den; a crow being 'bombed' by smaller redwing starlings. In real life, National Park and public land managers are faced with falling numbers of younger visitors, while those who do visit, have less understanding of why these places are special and how to appreciate them. If we are to stem this trend we need to start understanding nature's ways in our backyard, and we need to start early.

As many of us have grown up in urban environments and may not have spent a great amount of time in the outdoors, or might not have a back yard, where do we start to help our children develop that outdoor nature connection? Forget the textbooks and need to know names; that can come later. The rule with children age 5 and under is enthusiasm; if a child can sense this in adults they'll want to share that interest. Equally important is to understand that kids live their lives on a different scale. They revel in hands and knees contact with the micro-world. Wonder is found in the minute and at the simplest level.

Today's families are pulled in a hundred different directions, usually at the loss of access to natural places. But parents' motivation and willingness can make the difference in young people's lives. In this guide we highlight the fantastic free opportunities on our doorstep from bike trails to prairie dog towns, to playgrounds and creeks alive with bugs. The 1-5 year olds are (mostly) too young for organized activities, benefit from short trips close to home and get the most excitement from the simplest pebble searching, stick-poking activity. In this guide we show you how very easy it is to make the connection with the outdoor world at a time when it is most important for your child.

What is the extinction of a condor to a child who has never seen a wren?
Robert M Pyle

In the bigger picture, unless children have lots of outdoor play in woodland, ditch, creek or grassland there is little foundation to develop a connection with the natural environment. Without that connection, wild places become an abstraction for which they will have little empathy. Without empathy, how will children later in their lives truly engage on issues and choices about resource protection and sustainable futures? We want to nurture responsible young adults whose decisions and actions will affect people and our world in positive ways. How easy if parental responsibility simply boils down to getting our kids into the woods and creeks as often as we can!

Go explore with your child and have some fun!

Kathryn Pyke, October 2006.

Richard Louv's 'Last Child in the Woods—Saving Our Children from Nature Deficit Disorder' (Algonquin Books, 2005).
The Centers for Disease Control (CDC) reports that the US population of overweight children between ages two and five increased by almost 36% from 1989-1999, with two out of ten of America's children listed as clinically obese. This study also found that the amount of TV that children watched directly correlated with measures of their body fat. Experts now say (The Lancet, Anderson L.B et al., July 2006) that children need at least 90 minutes of exercise a day. U.S. pediatricians now provide standard advice that the under 5 age group should not spend more than 2 hours watching TV or playing electronic games if such trends are to be reversed.

> To a person uninstructed in natural history, his country or seaside stroll is a walk through a gallery filled with wonderful works of art, nine-tenths of which have their faces turned to the wall.
>
> *Thomas Huxley*

WHY 'PLAY' IN NATURE IS GOOD FOR HEALTHY CHILD DEVELOPMENT
- Group play in nature is based more on language skills, creativity and inventiveness and builds self-confidence. In contrast, organized sports and activities lend to social standing based more on age and physical competence.
- Children are more creative and imaginative in nature play.
- The physical and emotional exercise that children enjoy when they play in nature is more varied and less time-bound than organized sports.
- Nature play arouses children's senses and an awareness of the world around them.
- Nature demonstrates that diversity and balance are essential elements of sustainable life.

> Everybody has a ditch, or ought to. For only the ditches—and the fields, the woods, the ravines—can teach us to care enough for all the land.
>
> *Everybody's Ditch. From 'The Thunder Tree' by Robert Michael Pyle, 1993*

FINDING A SPECIAL PLACE FOR NATURE PLAY
Expeditions to mountains or National Parks may pale in comparison to the dugout in the weeds or leaves beneath a backyard willow, the rivulet of a seasonal creek, the ditch between a front yard and the road—all of these places are entire universes to children; they hold wonder and intimacy throughout the year and are places of initiation. If your child does not have such a place then look for one in your neighborhood. Get to know 10 square yards at the edge of a pond, field or yard. Look for the edges between habitats where field stops and tree begins, where bank and shoreline become pond. Life is always at the edges. Go regularly. Sit; watch and wait.

> It is not half so important to know as to feel when introducing a young child to the natural world.
>
> *Rachel Carson*

TIPS FOR HELPING CHILDREN CONNECT WITH NATURE
- **Keep it fun** and prepare to get muddy.
- **Share a child's wonder** at what they see; whether in a patch of grass or a special pebble.
- **Help a child develop observation skills** by watching what a bug does or where it goes; ant hills and turned over stones make good resources.
- **Go at a kid's pace** and let the adventure happen. If they get sidetracked by a beetle rather than fishing in one spot, let them follow their fun. Expect short attention spans.
- **Appeal to the senses of a child**—feel different textures that are slimy, oozy, soft, rough, and cold. Smell pine needles, crushed leaves, wet grass, and fungi. Listen for sounds of a scolding squirrel, bird

calls, and wind in the trees. Look for color, patterns, features on a plant or bug, or insect burrows under a stone. Taste chokecherry berries or a dandelion leaf and make pine needle or wild raspberry tea*.
- **Get down to a child's level.** Children revel in the minute; crouching or sitting with them allows better communication and can help with focusing on something for longer.
- **Don't just go out in perfect weather.** Visit your favorite field, ditch, stream or wood through all the seasons and become intimately acquainted with change and what makes these places special.
- **Think about your conversations**. Instead of trying to answer all those 'What's this?' questions, turn them around to 'What do you think? What does it look like? What is it doing?'
- **What fires your kid's imagination?** Tell your child you're going to your local park or playground and you may not get the enthusiastic response you hoped for. Instead try a themed trip to capture their imagination by posing it as a grasshopper or pebble hunt, stick collecting, stream hopping, tree climbing, mud pie digging trip etc. and you'll be surprised at their change in attitude.

*Caution on tasting plants: Learn to recognize Poison Hemlock (Conium maculatum) found near ditches and streams throughout Colorado which can be mistaken for fennel, parsley or wild carrot. The entire plant is poisonous and can be fatal to young children. Also help your child recognize Poison Ivy (Rhus radicans)—'Leaves of three, let it be'.

> If a child is to keep alive his inborn sense of wonder, he, or she, needs the companionship of at least one adult who can share it, rediscovering with him the joy, excitement, and mystery of the world we live in.
>
> *Rachel Carson*

BUILD ON AN INTEREST

- Go outside with different family members and family friends. Adults have as many different enthusiasms for the outdoors as kids, and each interaction will only build on a young child's outdoor experience.
- Read about nature or outdoor things. Follow up on something you saw and get a book out of the library to learn more, whether it's on worms, ants, or making your own bow and arrow; kid's books just get better and better with large format photographs and great selections.
- Spend time together drawing or painting nature—lay down the colors of a particular place or captures shapes by drawing round leaves or stones.
- Sign up for kid's nature programs e.g. 'Toddler Times' at Lookout Mountain Nature Center (pg 136) or the 'Just for Kids' programs by the City of Boulder (pg 34). These are free and great fun.
- Take a picture of a child doing something they really enjoy whether it's climbing a tree, getting muddy around a stream or showing off a bug in their bug box. Young kids can forget how much fun they had, but they never forget if they have that picture.

INSTILLING INSTINCTUAL CONFIDENCE THROUGH EXPOSURE TO RISK

Playing in wilder areas can pose an element of risk; uneven surfaces and rough vegetation lend themselves to bumps and scrapes, but your child is also exposed to a more complex environment. Natural places require problem solving and decision skills even at the simplest level: How to step across a stream? Cross these rocks? Children learning in these environments become wiser and build confidence for encountering such experiences on their own. Environments with open water, ice and rock can be irresistible. Kids will benefit from familiarity with such places through early parental guidance. Reduce your child's risk level by letting him or her explore on their own but by keeping them in sight.

THE PARADOX AND LEAVE NO TRACE ETHICS

Ask an outdoor lover about things they liked to do as a kid and many will refer to building dens, making a rickety tree house and damming a stream. Many of these projects will have involved bits of old wood, carpet and other things found nearby or salvaged from trash. Yet how many of these structures are tolerated or allowed (on liability grounds alone) in our neighborhood parks and local spaces? Here lies the paradox. Some of the most fun things identified by kids to do in the outdoors can also be environmentally destructive. Yet it is the process of project building in the outdoors that gives the hours of sensory exposure and helps seed that empathy and sense of connection.

For the under 5's some of the most popular and simplest activities such as getting to the edge of a stream or lake, exploring a clump of trees, making collections of natural things, to throwing sticks and stones do have impacts and can be a departure (see ethics marked with *) from Leave No Trace outdoor ethics. Parents are presented with the dilemma of how to teach Leave No Trace while still nurturing the sense of discovery and wonder that can only be obtained from doing some of the things mentioned above.

Leave No Trace Outdoor Ethics for Open Space
see www.LNT.org
- **Leave It As You Find It**
- **Stick to trails**
- Know Before You Go
- Trash Your Trash
- Pick Up Poop
- Be Careful With Fire
- Keep Wildlife Wild
- Share Our Trails and Manage Your Pet

The answer lies in the degree in which the activities are carried out. Parents need to be aware of harmful actions in natural areas, but can also gently guide activities to do the least harm. Areas with water are often the most problematic; water margins are fragile and wildlife easily disturbed.

Tread lightly, steer gently
- Select access points to rivers and streams that cause the least trampling to bank sides or vegetation; look for solid surfaces such as spillways, stepping stones, sand, gravel or stone-reinforced areas.
- If you've disturbed soil or rocks, try to return them to their original place and angle.
- Pick only the most common or abundant leaves for games, art projects and play.
- Leave the place of your adventure better than the way you found it.

Most parents will say that kids quickly relate to outdoor ethics if they are shown how. They soon learn to wonder at, and follow bugs, than capture and crush, to pick up trash than discard, to look after fishing tackle and pick up some discarded line for good measure, to build a campfire properly and understand what will or won't burn. Kids long remember when they've done something right that somebody else has done wrong.

> It is through close and intimate contact with a particular patch of ground that we learn to respond to the earth, to see that it really matters. We need to recognize the humble places where this alchemy occurs, and treat them as well as we treat out parks and preserves—or better, with less interference.
>
> *Robert M Pyle*

MAKE A PLEA TO PARKS AND RECREATION DEPARTMENTS

Parks and Recreation planners are under pressure. Demand for playing fields is up, while budget expenditure on parks is falling*. The resulting flat patch of grass may be perfect for organized sports, but not for unstructured or nature play. Watch any group of kids and see that when they are left to their own devices, they are drawn to the rough edges of such parks; the ditches, and rocky inclines, the natural vegetation. A park may be neatly trimmed and landscaped but the natural corners and edges where children like to play are lost in the process.

Saving our children from Nature Deficit Disorder requires parks to be planned as much for wild play opportunities and nature experiences, as for formal playground and ball fields. For example, management practices can be adjusted (change short grass mowing regimes for short cut loops through tall meadow borders). Or in the Design Phase, select trees and shrubs for imaginative play (such as silken seed heads and rattling pods) and to attract insects and butterflies.

(From 1981 to 1997 the amount of time children spent in organized sports increased by 27%. The US Youth Soccer Association has over 3 million members compared to 100,000 in 1974.)

THE FUTURE-GREEN URBAN DESIGN

Helping future generations rediscover nature means doing more than preserving essentially islands of wild land, parks and preserves. A healthy urban environment requires natural corridors for movement and genetic diversity. The challenge is to apply this principal to entire urban regions, where corridors for wildlife and consequently wild places extend deep into the heart of urban areas and are within a short walk of every child.

Although seemingly utopian, strategic planning through local authority Master Plans could incorporate mini greencorridors between every piece of common land, park or open space and in turn be linked at a county (and neighboring county) level. Just as bike paths are being developed into regional and local networks, so could the mini green corridor network.

Another call is for the creation of city farms or farm projects open to the public as an education resource. How many countless children's stories are based on pictures of the small family farm with a red barn? In reality, kids rarely get close to a real cow or see chickens kept for eggs. Surely here is one of the biggest disconnects that a City can begin to address even at the most modest level. There are some great examples in the private sector e.g. Haystack Mountain Goat Dairy in Boulder that allows free access (pg41), but it would be exemplary to see such facilities recognized in strategic plans.

WHAT'S HAPPENING NOW?

There is already an undercurrent of change in City of Boulder's parks and playgrounds. City planners are beginning to take a closer look at the 'Commons' or City open spaces in consultation with the community. Look for the Parks and Recreation Master Plan due out at the time of publication of this guide. This will list plans and changes in management at Parks and open spaces. Parents wishing to get more closely involved and see further change in facilities and management should attend public meetings, join (or sit in) on City Parks and Recreation Committees and comment as individuals and through community groups and housing associations. Please also consider getting involved with local non-profit groups that support our community efforts (such as Growing Gardens pg 66).

HOW TO USE THIS GUIDE

This guide is all about going outside, having fun and getting close to nature. It is also about using local parks and places within neighborhoods, some of which will hopefully be in walking or cycling distance from your home.

PURPOSE OF THIS GUIDE
1. Become aware of the importance of play in nature.
2. Find a fun and appropriate location for your family outing.
2. Know what to expect when you get there so you can plan what to bring.
3. Develop an intimate knowledge i.e. sense of place, of the parks and open space in your neighborhood.
4. Enjoy natural places in different ways to increase your child's understanding and appreciation.

ABOUT THE LOCATIONS
Locations described in this guide have been picked with some or all of the following qualities:
- Short travel distance
- Play areas set well back from busy roads
- Ample parking
- Quiet environments
- Natural settings
- Fun or unusual features
- Water aspect (stream, river, creek, pond, lake)
- Good for wildlife experiences or for seeing a particular animal
- 'Add on' sites e.g. playground next to a wood or creek
- Short hikes or bike rides with lots of stopping points
- Options for different activities
- Sites to appeal to the senses
- Sites that stimulate an inquisitive mind
- Educational value

To be rooted is perhaps the most important but least understood need of the human soul.

Simone Weil

tasting chokecherry berries

USING THE SUMMARY BOX INFORMATION

Each of the 51 locations listed in this guide begins with a summary box covering the following:
Address, telephone number and web site. Information on nearly every site in this guide can be found using the telephone numbers and/or web sites listed. Some websites provide more information (others less) than described in this guide.
Charges, entrance fees and hours of opening. Correct as of 'going to press time', open hours are listed for Visitor Centers and Museums; these may change—check before going. Virtually all the sites described in this guide are free with the exception of parking charges for some State Parks and city-managed wildlife areas. Expect to see fees for some sites listed under 'Other Options'; for example where swimming pools are described.

Directions.
   Golden: Directions are given from Golden Visitor Center in Downtown Golden at 1010 Washington Avenue, Golden Colorado 80401; 303 279 3113 www.goldencochamber.org. Note that Hwy6 is also signed 'West 6th Avenue' at the junction with 19th Street and should not be confused with the West 6th Avenue frontage road serving Jefferson County Fairgrounds.
   Boulder: Directions are given from Broadway or the nearest arterial road.
Mileage and distance. Different sized tires can give different mileage readings. Therefore look for turns and endpoints 0.1-0.2 miles above or below the given figure to allow for discrepancies.

Public/Alternative Transportation.
   Boulder: Many locations in this guide are served by bus routes. Where possible route numbers are provided. The SKIP bus runs north/south on Broadway, and the HOP loops through Boulder past Pearl Street Mall and CU Campus. For more detailed information see www.bouldercolorado.gov under 'Alternative Transportation'. This helpful site lists descriptions, schedules and a link to www.RTD-denver.com
   Golden: Golden is less well served by public transportation so fewer bus routes are listed. Golden Visitor Center on Washington Avenue and 10th Street provides schedules and a RTD self-guide computer information station. Note: Boulder and Golden downtowns are linked by express bus route service GS (weekdays only).
   Bike Lanes and Multi-use Paths: Bike route maps and information can be found on both City of Golden and City of Boulder websites.
Parking. Where possible number of vehicle spaces are provided. Locations that fill quickly are noted and alternatives given.
Restrooms. Caring for small children means you take a greater interest in restroom facilities than you would as an adult. Vault restrooms tend to be found on open space land away from water lines. Hygiene standards can vary and the deep drop pit may not be an option on the grounds of safety and ease of use with young children. Port-a-potty restrooms present similar issues. For this reason all types of restrooms are listed. 'Fully equipped restrooms' refer to flush toilets with sinks and running water. Many locations in this guide do not have restrooms; even if they do, they may not be suitable for use for reasons described above. To cope with small children's bathroom needs, consider carrying a potty in your car.
Water. Being thirsty can mean an early end to an outing. Drinking fountains are listed but take note of seasonal operation. Most drinking fountains are disconnected during the winter to prevent freeze damage. Where we note 'summer only' expect fountains to operate from late April to the end of September.

Perennial Sweet Pea

Dogs: Boulder: Dogs are required to be on-leash in the City of Boulder including Parks and Recreation areas and on paved multi-use trails. City of Boulder Open Space and Mountain Parks has areas where dogs are prohibited, on-leash, and where they can be off-leash under voice and sight control. In designated voice and sight control locations, visitors with dogs must meet the requirements of the new 'Voice and Sight Control Dog Tag Program' introduced 8.7.06 (see www.osmp.org). Dogs not displaying tags representing participation in the Dog Tag Program must be on leash. Some trailheads require dogs to be kept on leash in the parking areas and a short distance along the trail as signed.

Golden: Dogs are required to be on-leash in the City of Golden (including all City parks and trails) and on all Jefferson County Open Space property.

Dog Parks: Both Golden and Boulder provide City-managed Dog Parks where dogs can run off leash in a designated area. These are becoming increasingly popular with some dog parks listed in this guide. For more information on Dog Parks and leash guidelines visit City of Boulder and City of Golden websites: www.bouldercolorado.gov and www.ci.golden.co.us.

Season. Colorado's low rainfall and climate means that most days can be outdoor days. However that still means it can be hot, cold or sometimes very windy. Seasonal advice is provided for each site including shade and sheltered areas as well as winter warmth. On bad weather or marginal days, the locations with museums or visitor centers make good choices. They are also backed up with outdoor options if the weather picks up.

OTHER OPTIONS

This separate section briefly lists nearby sites that may also be of interest with younger children.

OUTDOOR CONSIDERATIONS

Location choice—Cater to the age(s) of your children and their interests. Note busy and quiet times for visits and plan accordingly.

Weather—Check the forecast and plan where to go and what to bring. Consider whether you want an open, sheltered or shaded option.

Sun protection—Wear a high SPF sunscreen, even in winter and keep a spare tube in your bag. Get your kids used to wearing hats, and shirts at swimming/splashing places; it reduces the amount of sunscreen you need to use and better protects their skin.

Clothing—Bring clothing for layering from hot to cold situations and keep a spare change in your vehicle.

Food and drink—Always bring food. It's amazing how many outings have been saved from hunger and tantrums with a packet of crackers. Stash an extra pack in your vehicle for when you forget or run out of food.

Water—Always bring something to drink. Cycling bottles are fairly spill proof, and easy to carry. Take extra water in the car for those times you forget to bring it along or run out. Gallon containers are good for water storage and handy for when you need to wash a child down.

Sticky situations—In addition to the ever-handy wipes, a washcloth and paper towel are great for ice cream eating and other mopping up episodes.

First aid—Band aids, antibiotic cream with pain reliever and some candy can go a long way towards soothing small scrapes and cuts and can avoid heading home prematurely.

Equipment, props and toys—Check your location for whether you want to bring balls, kites, bikes and other play equipment. Sand toys and a few plastic sealable containers in the car are handy for just about every excursion. Bug boxes, butterfly nets, and even magnifying glasses may at times seem a little contrived, but can provide a great focus for a nature outing. Don't forget the fishing rod and tackle box for most water locations.

ACKNOWLEDGEMENTS

Jenny Stein, 2nd Editor
Matt Claussen, Conservation Coordinator, City of Boulder Parks and Recreation
Steve Amstead, Ranger Supervisor, City of Boulder Open Space and Mountain Parks
Burton Stoner, Ranger, City of Boulder Open Space and Mountain Parks
Shawn Sprenger, City of Golden Parks and Recreation
Brenda Porter, Education Director, Colorado Mountain Club
Susy Levin Alkaitis, Deputy Director, Leave No Trace—Center for Outdoor Ethics

PHOTOGRAPHIC

Dana Abrahamson—Historic Evergreen, Inc. Dulce Aldama—CU Natural History Museum. Kristie Brice. Peter Butler—Lyons Sculpture Trail. Ramona Clark—Growing Gardens. Cherie Duge Paul. Gale Elstun. Nigel Gregory. Margaret Josey-Parker. Scott Joy. Povy Kendal Atchison. Cathy Kowitz. Stacy Lambright—Boulder County Resource Conservation Division. Susy Levin Alkaitis. Jason Manke. Joy Masters—City of Boulder Parks and Recreation. Julie Messa. Andrew and Joan Terrill. Back Cover Credits: Margaret Josey-Parker and Suzy Levin Alkaitis.

Thanks to our young photo stars! Alec and Ella; Isabelle and Walter; Zane, Jared and Carly; Max and Sam; Quintan and Tess; Oz, Noah and Pharoah; Iona; Gabriel and Nadine; Noah; Jaegar and Nyneve; Ali and Arian; the Abrahamsons and the Werlins; Catherine and Rachel; Quinn, Ava and Clair; Julian and Simone; Anna and Addie. Riley, Micheal and Payshe. Ryan. The Lambrights.

A NOTE ON SAFETY

Safety is an important concern in all outdoor activities. No guidebook can alert you to every hazard. When you visit any of the locations described in this guide, you assume responsibility for your own safety and that of your party. Some details may have changed in this book since it was written. Always check posted signs and exercise common sense.

A NOTE ON GUIDEBOOK INFORMATION AND ACCURACY

Every effort has been made to ensure the accuracy of information in this guide at the time of going to print. On a number of pages we highlight locations where change to facilities or access will occur. Expect some changes as you use this guide (hopefully only for the better) and please let us know of any changes via our website at www.wolverinepublishing.com.

1 ANN U. WHITE TRAIL

This child-sized, pristine canyon makes a perfect getaway with the under 5's. Follow the easy creek-side trail for as little or as far as you want. Listen to the wind in the trees, the chattering of mountain chickadees and the cascading whistles of canyon wrens. Play around large boulders and dabble in the trickling creek. Bring a picnic and plan to spend some time in this quiet and beautiful location.

Ann U. White Trail
Fourmile Canyon Creek

Pinto Drive, Boulder 80304
Boulder County Parks and Open Space
303 441 3950
www.co.boulder.co.us/openspace

Location: 2.3 miles from Broadway and Lee Hill Drive.

Directions: From the intersection of Broadway, and Lee Hill Drive, drive west for 1.1 miles. Turn left onto Wagonwheel Gap Road. Turn left just after Bow Mountain Road into Pinto Drive. Follow this 'No Outlet' road on a dirt track to its end.

Parking: There are five designated spaces at the end of this quiet residential drive, with a strict tow policy if you park anywhere else. If the parking lot is full, drive back to Wagonwheel Gap Road and look for roadside parking eastwards. Consider bringing a bike in a two adult party, so that you can drop the kids at the trailhead, find parking and then cycle back quickly to your party. There are 4 bike racks at the trailhead entrance.

Season: All year with good fall color. This canyon is very sheltered with plenty of shade. A good option for a high wind day.

Restrooms: No.

Water: No. Bring your own.

Dogs: Yes. On-leash.

Looking at horsetails

It's hard to believe that you can find such a quiet and special location as Fourmile Canyon Creek so close to urban Boulder. The trail is named after Ann U. White, an environmentalist, local resident and champion of open space. White loved to walk the canyon in all seasons with her family. She led efforts to preserve Fourmile Creek Canyon in 1983 and donated an additional 20 acres of land adjacent to the trail.

The Ann U. White trail is 1.75 miles long (one way) and follows easy ground next to the trickling creek (seasonal flow) with only a slight incline, for most of its length. At times the trail twists and narrows with occasional small granite walls providing an element of surprise. Perhaps most captivating of all is that this landscape does not tower and intimidate, but is on an altogether smaller and more inviting scale for small people. Don't expect crowds; the parking policy means you are unlikely to meet more than a handful of people at this location which all adds to the element of seclusion. However, do expect the sounds of nature, whether it's wind, water or birds, within a few steps of the trailhead.

Tips: Bring food and water. Visit the Ann U. White Trail mid-week or at non-peak weekend times to avoid parking hassles. Pack old shoes in case feet go in the creek. Watch for poison ivy.

Other options:

1. Fourmile Creek Trailhead. Is your dog fed up of being on a leash? Visit the new fenced Dog Park at Foothills Community Park via a pleasant 5-10min walk from Fourmile Creek Trailhead. The trailhead is located on the south side of West Lee Hill Drive, 0.4 miles from its intersection with Broadway. There is parking for about 40 vehicles. You can see the Dog Park from the parking lot. Follow the level gravel Foothills Trail southwards. After a few minutes the trail crosses the Fourmile Creek drainage via a small footbridge—a good stopping point for inquisitive kids with its large cottonwood trees in otherwise open grassland. Look for the prairie dog colony on the west side of the trail.

Fourmile Creek Canyon lies in the transition zone between the grasslands of the high plains and the coniferous forests of the Rocky Mountain Front Range. At the trailhead pick up a brochure that provides checklist information by season on the hundreds of plants, birds and animals recorded in the canyon. Choose to explore at the pace of your toddler or older child, or bring a child carrier. If you have a stroller, you'll need to lift it over a low entrance bar, but the first 200 yards of the trail is smooth and wide enough for good access. After this point, the path narrows and becomes a little rockier.

As you walk the trail, peek around large boulders, and feel the textures of the lichens and mosses. Up in the Ponderosa pines look for stripped bark showing where porcupines have been feeding. At the base look for piles of pine cone fragments indicating black Abert's squirrels have been feasting. Sights, sounds and experiences will vary with each season at Fourmile Creek Canyon. Enjoy immersing your kids in this special place.

2 ARAPAHOE RIDGE PARK

How can any child resist a child-sized mound of rocks and tunnels made for climbing and wriggling through? Visit this park for sheer novelty. If you still have the energy, and school is not in session, choose from all shapes and sizes of play structures in the open access grounds of Eisenhower Elementary School.

Arapahoe Ridge Park ('Rock Park')

Eisenhower Drive, Boulder 80303
City of Boulder Parks and Recreation Department
303 413 7200
www.bouldercolorado.gov

Location: 2.8 miles east of Broadway and Arapahoe Avenue.

Public Transportation: RTD Bus, No. 206, stops by the park and elementary school on Eisenhower Drive.

Directions: Drive east on Arapahoe Avenue for 2.4 miles. Turn right onto 48th Street for 0.1 miles. 48th Street turns into Eisenhower Drive; continue for 0.2 miles until just before Eisenhower Elementary School. The sign for the park is on the left side of the road in front of the school tennis courts. Either park on Eisenhower near the entrance sign, or look for the dead-end residential street, Kellogg Circle (this road is just north of the park sign, at about 2.7 miles, on the left side of Eisenhower). Go to the end of Kellogg Circle to a visitor parking area.

Parking: Kellogg Circle provides a quiet paved parking area in a residential street for approximately 8-10 cars. This street backs onto Arapahoe Ridge Park, and is 50 yards from the play structure. Eisenhower Drive can be a busy road to park on, but as a first time visitor, parking close to the entrance sign ensures you have located this park.

Season: All year. Warm and sheltered in winter.
Restrooms: No.
Water: No. Bring water.
Dogs: Yes. On-leash.

A visit to check out the rock mound and tunnel feature at Arapahoe Ridge Park is well worth it for sheer novelty value. Built as a central open space feature in a planned housing development over 30 years ago, cul-de-sac residential streets back onto this open space. This provides a quiet location set well back from any busy roads although somewhat hard to find.

From the entrance sign follow the paved path along a narrow corridor for 200 yards until you reach the center of the park and the location of the play area.

The rock feature (approximately 15 x 25 foot width) is built out of natural sandstone and cleverly designed for climbing on the outside and crawling through short tunnels within. The potential for scrambling and peek-a boo is endless. This feature was primarily built for the under 5's, so if you're a few years older you will be too big to fit through!

Other play features include hand-operated diggers (pea gravel base) next to a cave area, a metal roundabout, infant swings and a small ramp and slide structure. A shelter with picnic tables is located next to the play area.

There is a 0.2 mile paved loop around the edge of the park for easy bike riding and large mown grass areas good for ball games.

Tips: Bring water, a bike or trike, and good scrambling shoes. A hand held flashlight might be fun for shining into nooks and crannies in the stone tunnels; maybe you'll find an ant or beetle.

Other options:
1. Eisenhower Elementary School Playgrounds. Explore the rest of the open space area behind Eisenhower Elementary School. There is a great variety of play structures and swings. If school is not in session enjoy open access from the park.

3 BOULDER RECYCLING

For something completely different make a visit to the state-of-the-art Boulder County Recycling Center. Find the right hole to drop-off your recyclables, marvel at giant bales of plastic bottles and cardboard, see recycling operations in action from a walkway and look for wildlife in the large cattail ponds on site. Plenty to stimulate the senses and learn even from the briefest visit.

Boulder County Recycling Center

1901 63rd Street, Boulder 80301
Education Visitor Center:
720 564 2220
www.bouldercountyrecycles.net

Open Hours: Recycling Drop-off Center: 24 hours Education Center : Monday-Friday 8am-4:30pm. Closed holidays.
Location: 4.1 miles from Broadway and Arapahoe Avenue.
Directions: Drive east on Arapahoe Avenue for 3.8 miles. Turn left onto S.63rd Street marked by a small green sign for the Recycling Center and Stazio Recreation Complex. Drive 0.3 miles over 2 sets of railroad tracks until you see the entrance for the Recycling Center on your left.
Parking: Designated parking for recycling just after you turn in the entrance. Check website for list of accepted materials. For the Education Center, and to look at the wildlife ponds, follow signs for 'Visitor Parking' along the north side of the Center, to 2 large paved parking lots at the west end of the site.
Season: All year.
Restrooms: Fully equipped restrooms with wheelchair access inside the Education Center. None outside.
Water: Drinking fountains inside the Education Center. No water outside.
Dogs: No.

GALE ELSTUN

Although this may not be the most obvious recreation outing, there's plenty at the Boulder County Recycling Center to fascinate. If you spend just a few minutes in the drop-off area of Boulder County Recycling Center, you'll realize that recycling is a family activity—notice how the younger kids love finding the right bin. Combine this with a tour of the Center, viewing recycling sorting on the conveyor belts, and enjoying the peaceful grounds of the ponds and wetlands at the north side of the site, and you have plenty of interest to make a good outing with young children.

Boulder County Recycling Center was opened in 2001 and provides local residents with a state-of-the-art processing plant and education resource. (Locals may also be interested to know that in partnership with local community-based organizations, the City of Boulder is striving to be a Zero Waste community, joining a handful of other such cities across the United States. For more information visit www.ecocyle.org.)

For your visit bring a box-full of recyclables. If your kids are interested show them the different bins and pick up some brochures from the information area to learn more. From this location you may see containers of recyclable material being taken to the unloading bays, and bales of sorted materials

GALE ELSTUN

Tips: Bring a box of recyclables to unload into the recycle bins. Bring some binoculars for a close up view of the recycling operations and to watch birds on the wildlife ponds.

Other options:

1. Guided Tours of the Recycling Center. For dates and times of free, guided tours visit www.bouldercountyrecycles.net or call 720 564 2220.

2. South Teller Trailhead. Visit this trailhead for a quiet trip into prairie and farmland with opportunities to see horses, llamas and prairie dogs. The Trailhead is located west of 95th Street on the north side of Arapahoe Road. Facilities at the parking lot include vault restrooms, picnic tables and an accessible fishing pier on Teller Lake. The Teller Farm Trail is 2.3 miles long and links to the North Teller Trailhead on Valmont Road along an easy dirt trail. The site is exposed with little shade. Avoid hot sunny days.

ready for truck shipment to the side of the site.

The Education Center is located at the far end of the property in a surprisingly peaceful setting of wildlife ponds with a striking backdrop of Longs Peak and the Front Range foothills to the west. Pause outside the Center to look at the 'How to Compost' exhibits and learn about backyard and worm composting. Walk through the Native Plant Garden and discover the beautiful plants that grow naturally in Colorado. Inside, take a self-guided tour of the recycling displays (bold and colorful) and follow this up by taking the walkway to get views of recycling operations up close. Kids will enjoy seeing the different materials being sorted from conveyor belts and the huge bays of bottles and crushed glass.

For a contrast to your recycling visit look for wildlife around the wetland areas and ponds. Although there is no trail, there is good viewing from the raised pond sides. The ponds are alive from February through late fall with activity from Red-winged Blackbirds. The distinctive red patches on the bird's wings, their aggressive defense of nesting areas and loud call make them easy viewing for children. During summer months watch the hovering and chasing antics of dragonflies and damselflies.

4 BOULDER CREEK

Rushing water, cool underpasses, and lots of wading and picnicking make Boulder Creek Path between City Park and the Kid's Fishing Ponds one of the most popular family outings in Boulder. Bring a bike, stroller, or simply walk choosing from options such as hands-on crafts at the Boulder's Farmer's Market, side trips to playgrounds or exploring the wooded paths around the Kid's Fishing Ponds and playing next to creek-side sculptures. Always something to distract or amuse, and despite its popularity, plenty of quiet places to linger.

Boulder Creek—Farmer's Market to Evert Pierson Kid's Fishing Ponds

13th Street to 6th Street, Boulder 80302
City of Boulder Parks and Recreation
303 413 7200
www.bouldercolorado.gov

Location: One block east of Broadway and Arapahoe Avenue.

Public Transportation: RTD bus services stop on Broadway less than 100 yards from 13th street and also along Canyon Boulevard close to the Creek Trail and Fishing Ponds.

Directions: 13th Street and City Park are located between Arapahoe Avenue and Canyon Boulevard, one block east of Broadway.

Parking: Parking can be difficult around City Park and the Broadway/Boulder Creek area. If possible bike, walk or bus from a convenient location. At weekends there is limited parking for Boulder County Farmer's Market just off Canyon Boulevard and 14th Street in the City Lots. Two blocks to the west free parking is available on weekends next to Boulder Public Library off Arapahoe Avenue and 11th Street, and by the City offices off Canyon Boulevard and 11th Street. If these locations are full see www.farmersmarket.org for further parking options or find metered or free parking on nearby streets.

Evert Pierson Kid's fishing ponds.

P robably Boulder's best-known path, the Boulder Creek Trail, although often very busy on the paved section, has lots to offer and plenty of quiet, out of the way places for playing with kids and exploring the river.

Described is the section of the trail west from 13th Street (home of Boulder County Farmer's Market) through to the Evert Pierson Kid's Fishing Ponds located behind Boulder Courthouse buildings just off Canyon Boulevard and 6th Street. Throughout this section, there are interpretative signs themed on creek wildlife and many places for getting wet. Enjoy the different temperatures, sounds and changes in light along the trail as you duck under the street underpasses.

City Park is the name given to the open space area that encompasses 13th Street Community Plaza, Boulder Museum of Contemporary Art (BMoCA), Boulder Dushanbe Teahouse, the Band Shell and old steam train. Popular at all times of the year, this area throngs with people on Saturday mornings when the farmers market is in full swing offering a good range of fresh and locally grown produce as well as other tempting foods. Kid-friendly attractions range from live music in two different areas, face painting and the balloon man, and the free Art Stop located outside the BMoCA entrance. Here kids can get hands-on experience making artwork related to the Museum's exhibitions (see www.bmoca.org). The program runs from 9am-1pm, caters to ages 2-12, and kids get to sit down at tables in the shade ending

For the Evert Pierson Fishing Ponds, plenty of free weekend space is available in the Boulder Justice Center parking lot off Canyon Boulevard and 6th Street (Note: this is not available midweek) and on nearby residential streets. For midweek parking the following hourly charge options are available: At the library parking lot off Arapahoe with a 3 hour limit, or in the 15th Street Parking Garage, between Pearl Street and Canyon Boulevard.

Season: All year round. Plenty of shade from tall trees on hot days. Look for ice on the Fishing Ponds in winter.

Restrooms: Nearest public restrooms from 13th Street are located three blocks north at 13th Street and Pearl Street Mall. Restrooms are also available at Eben G. Fine Park. On Saturdays, Boulder Museum of Contemporary Art on 13th Street makes its facilities available for public use. Boulder Public Library also has public restrooms. All these locations are fully equipped and wheelchair accessible.

Water: Drinking fountains are located at the restrooms described above. In addition a drinking fountain is located on the north side of Arapahoe Avenue and 13th Street next to the flood interpretation signs and footbridge to Andrew's Arboretum, and by the City building where the footbridge accesses the library off 11th.

Dogs: Yes, but not advised in the Farmer's Market. All other areas on-leash.

Drop into free "Artstop" sessions outside BMoCA

with a piece of art to take home. Entrance to art exhibits inside the museum is also free on Saturdays.

Just next to the Museum, look for the mountain lion marking the City of Boulder's education and outreach booth. Ask questions, pick up brochures and get to touch and hold some exhibits. Before leaving this area, take your kids over to the roses of Boulder Dushanbe Teahouse. The gardens of this hand crafted Tajikistan building contain over a hundred varieties of labeled heirloom and climbing roses that flower summer long. Take in the smell and color, but avoid the prickles.

Follow the trail west, under Broadway, to reach more City Open Space on both sides of the creek. The first footbridge to the left reaches a small older-style playground with 2 child and 2 tot swings, a metal slide, and 2 sit-and-scoop diggers in a pea gravel base. This is a quiet area with picnic tables, shade and creek access. Continue west on the paved trail to reach a Touch and Scent garden and a creek-side stone amphitheater that provides a good wading opportunity. You are now adjacent to Boulder Public Library parking lot where tall trees provide plenty of shade. If you or your kids have an interest in martial arts, continue towards the library and pause at the large paved area underneath the building. This is a popular summer location where disciplines with swords and sticks to the fluid hand and body movements of Tai Chi are taught and practiced. A few more yards to the west there is another quiet short grass area with a small sandy beach accessing the creek.

Cross a footbridge back to the north side of the Boulder Creek Trail. Unpaved trails run parallel through the woodland providing a break from the paved surface. Just west of the 9th Street underpass, pause to play chase around the metal sculptures in the Charles A. Haertling Sculpture Garden before arriving at the Fishing Ponds.

The **Evert Pierson Kids Fishing Ponds** are another of Boulder's great kid-friendly resources. Two large ponds with lush undergrowth and tall shade trees are regularly stocked with Rainbow Trout from Memorial Day through Labor Day. The great attraction is that only kids 12 and under can fish for them! Short inviting loops around the ponds are just the right length for an exploring toddler; look for the shaggy mats of red willow roots and ever present mallard ducks. Regularly spaced fishing piers make accessible fishing points for wheelchair users. Exploring around the back of the ponds gives more opportunities for creek access and splashing in a wilder setting. Step over the creek trail to check out the raised bed butterfly garden just in front of the Justice Center. Do you see any butterflies?

Other options:

1. Boulder Creek Trail Short Bike Links. From Broadway go west on the Creek Trail for just under one mile to reach Eben G. Park and playground (pg 52) Or go east for about one and half miles to reach Scott Carpenter Park off Arapahoe Avenue and 30th Street (pg 87).

2. Andrew's Arboretum. Located on the east side of Broadway between Grandview and Marine Streets. Often referred to by locals as Pizza Park (because of its proximity to a now long-gone pizza parlor), Andrew's Arboretum provides a peaceful haven in the heart of the City. Picnic and look at the different flowers, trees and leaves. The Arboretum was established in 1948 by Maud Reed, a botany teacher at Boulder High School. She used this land as an outdoor classroom; a role which is continued today in its management by City of Boulder as an education resource. Enjoy the shade, play along the paths and pick up a free Arboretum brochure which explains the different plants and trees.

3. Boulder Map Gallery. How many times have you wanted a map to locate that special place? This store stocks just about every local map (including great ones for the Front Range), as well as lots of poster and wall-size regional and world maps. If they don't stock what you want they'll know someone that does. The store is located at the southeast end of 13th Street Community Plaza.

4. Caught Out in Bad Weather? Visit the fish tank displays inside the main entrance of Boulder Public Library and then check out the children's book collections on the same floor.

Tips: Boulder County Farmer's Market dates: Saturdays 8am-2pm April 1 to Nov 4. Wednesdays 4pm-8pm May 10 to Oct 4. See www.boulderfarmers.org. At the Kid's Fishing Ponds look for the distinctive gray and white Belted Kingfisher often perched high on a tree branch intently watching the water for small fish. Don't forget to bring a net and bucket to look at water skippers and other pond creatures. Beware bikes and other fast traffic on the busy Boulder Creek Trail with toddlers.

5 CHAUTAUQUA PARK

A classic Boulder outing! Beautifully sited at the base of Boulder's Flatiron rock formations, Chautauqua Park has great charm and is beloved by many. Choose to hike, picnic, touch furry animals in the Ranger Cottage, explore the historic grounds, or dawdle in the playground under the shade of tall trees. A great outing for all ages.

Inside the Ranger Cottage with a fox pelt.

Chautauqua Park and Chautauqua Ranger Cottage
9th Street and Baseline Road, Boulder 80302
Chautauqua Park
303 442 3282
www.chautauqua.com
Chautauqua Meadow and Ranger Cottage
303 441 3440
www.bouldercolorado.gov

Open Hours: Ranger Cottage:10am-4pm daily in summer. Winter hours may vary, but generally Thursday through Sunday 10am-3pm

Location: 1 mile from Broadway and Baseline Road.

Public Transportation: There is an RTD bus stop close to the parking lot.

Directions: Drive west on Baseline Road for about 1 mile, and then turn left into Chautauqua Park at the signed entrance opposite Grant Place.

Parking: For the Ranger Cottage and closest access to the trailheads, turn immediately right inside the entrance into the paved parking lot where there is space for about 40 cars. For closer parking to the playground in Chautauqua Park, or if the trailhead parking is full, follow one way signs and look for parking along the road circling the open grass area. There is also parking behind the auditorium in the northeast of the park.

A picnic at Chautauqua Park on a lazy summer weekend is a quintessential Boulder experience. Families spread out on picnic blankets jostle with all ages of sunbathers, students and Frisbee players in a surprisingly peaceful medley. Choose from many options from taking your dog and child (probably in a back pack carrier) on one of the Flatirons trails, visiting the education exhibits at the Ranger Cottage, picnicking under the shade of large trees or dropping into the playground.

The Trails and Ranger Cottage (see above for open hours) are managed by City of Boulder Open Space and Mountain Parks. The Ranger Cottage is located at the south end of the parking lot and bordered by a native plants garden. The wide wrap-around porch of this historic building invites you to seek shade and enter the building. Enjoy the touch and feel animal skins, skulls and tracks; changes in 2007 will include the introduction of Touch Boxes and new displays. Rangers are present to help with questions on plants and wildlife and the Cottage is well-stocked with brochures. If you are new to the area,

Season: All year. Attractive in all seasons with plenty of shade from tall trees.

Restrooms: One fully equipped restroom with wheelchair access on the east side of the Ranger Cottage available year round during daylight hours. In the summer, public restrooms are available at ground level on the south side of Chautauqua Dining Hall about 100 yards from the playground.

Water: Drinking fountain located near the restroom on the south wall of the Ranger Cottage and to the east of the Chautauqua Dining Hall (summer only).

Dogs: Yes. On-leash in Chautauqua Park. For the City of Boulder trails there is a trailhead on-leash requirement for a short distance and then an off leash voice and sight control requirement.

pick up the Circle Hikes Guide (also available as a PDF on the City of Boulder web site) and choose a hike (see Other Options below), some starting at an easy 1.1 miles. If the Cottage is closed, orient yourself at the well-maintained information boards that provide clear maps of all the hikes available from the parking lot trailheads.

The grounds and buildings of Chautauqua Park are cared for by the Chautauqua Association, a movement begun in 1874 to promote educational experiences and enjoyment of the outdoors. This 26-acre site in Boulder is one of only 20 sites still operating nationwide (the number at the height of the Chautauqua heyday was 20,000!). In February 2006, Chautauqua's special status was noted with its designation as a National Historic Landmark, the first of its kind in the Denver Metro area. Today the park hosts many events including concerts, plays, films and lectures. See: www.chautauqua.com or call 303 442 3282 for information.

... a large Horse Chestnut tree near ...ing Hall. In fall collect the large shiny brown seeds—there are usually plenty to be found—and teach your kids to play the Olde English Game of Conkers. See www.woodlands-junior.kent.sch.uk/customs/conkers.html for more information. Chautauqua Park is busy on summer weekends; arrive early to get a parking space, or consider a trip by bike, foot or bus. Check out the Brunch Buffet in the elegant Dining Hall—open everyday from 8am-2pm. Don't forget your picnic blanket!

Explore the landscaped grounds, picnic and capture a sense of former days; original stone benches and shelters are still present and the historic cottages can be rented on a weekly basis. From the grass and open areas, move to the playground on the east side of the park. Enjoy the unusual miniature castle front that allows you to run through different entrances, as well as a slide built into an earth bank (watch out; it whooshes you down pretty fast!). Other more typical features include children and infant swings, a slide structure, large very polished boulders and a bus. A great aspect to this playground is the large elm tree which provides shade over much of the play area.

Looking For Conkers

McClintock Trail

Other options:

1. Short Loop Hikes from Chautauqua. A) McClintock Trail and Enchanted Mesa Trail Loop < 1mile. This short loop descends into lush woodland following a streamside trail (seasonal flow), then climbs gently to meet with the Enchanted Mesa Trail at the small stone bridge (watch for poison ivy here!). Follow the gravel fire road back to your start point. Start at the McClintock Trailhead at the picnic area on the south side of the Chautauqua auditorium. This is a great shaded hike for a hot day. Note: No dogs are allowed on the McClintock Trail. **B) Chautauqua Meadows Trail** < 1 mile. An open hike through Chautauqua Meadows with a chance to look for wildflowers and insects. Start at the centrally located Meadows Trailhead from the Ranger Cottage parking lot. Follow the Meadows Trail and then keep taking a series of right turns using well-defined paths to bring you back to your start point. Make the hike longer by heading out further west along the trail before turning right. Pick a calm day with pleasant temperatures, and bring a small container to look at bugs.

2. 'Natural Selections' Nature Hikes and Programs. The City of Boulder provides an all year, free education and nature program that includes specially designed children's activities. For the latest information visit the City web site: www.boulder-colorado.gov or use the quick link www.naturehikes.org which will get you to the same page. Look for programs marked 'Just for Kids' and check the recommended age. Topics can range from 'Old Man Coyote', to 'Music in the Meadows', to searching for all things beginning with the letter 'R' on open space.

6 COOT LAKE/TOM WATSON

Combine the best of the natural and the playground worlds all from one location. See prairie dogs in their true habitat along an interpretative trail, make a loop of Coot Lake or simply let the dog go swimming! Cross over the road for one of the best playgrounds in Boulder with lots of moving structures and a large grass area with good shade. Easy to find and perfect for picnicking and meeting with friends.

Coot Lake and Tom Watson Park

6180 North 63rd Street, Boulder 80503
City of Boulder Parks and Recreation
303 413 7200
www.bouldercolorado.gov

Location: 0.9 miles from the Diagonal Highway.

Directions: From Diagonal Highway exit north on 63rd Street. Drive for about 0.9 miles. Coot Lake is on the west side of the road. Tom Watson Park is directly opposite on the east side of the road. Drive 100 yards further north on 63rd Street and turn right into IBM Park Road. The parking lot is the first right.

Parking: Coot Lake has 10 vehicle parking spaces. If this is full, park at the Tom Watson Park paved parking area where there is room for over 100 vehicles. Access Coot Lake by the footpath from the south end of the parking lot.

Season: All year. Tom Watson Park is sheltered. Coot Lake and the adjacent loop trails are more exposed. Avoid hot or high wind days to do the prairie dog loop.

Restrooms: Tom Watson Park: Large fully equipped restrooms with wheelchair access open year round. Restrooms include 3 shower cubicles. At Coot Lake: Two vault restrooms near parking lot and two port-a-potty toilets (summer only) located on the prairie dog outer loop trail.

Water: Drinking fountains are located inside the restrooms at Tom Watson Park. Open year round. No water in the Coot Lake section.

Dogs: Dogs can swim off leash in Coot Lake but must be under voice and sight control. In Tom Watson Park they must be on-leash.

The Tom Watson/Coot Lake location provides kids with contrasting experiences between a formal park and a natural wildlife area. Yet the two areas can be accessed and enjoyed in one trip simply by walking the few yards across 63rd Street. Visit this one location with plenty of time to explore, or visit different parts over repeat trips throughout the seasons.

Tom Watson Park saw major refurbishment in 2003 and is now a designated City Park. The large playground forms the main focus of the park, set amid tall trees and spacious short turf areas. There are too many structures to list, but what is striking about the Kompan design play equipment is the amount of moving things; from modern look roundabouts and spiraling poles to a four-person seesaw. Other structures include a ramp and slide structure, a twisting rope climbing apparatus, a sand pouring station and periscope. There is plenty to keep most under 5's happy and for several hours. On hot days escape the heat to the southwest corner of the park where there are large trees and picnic tables or

use the group shelter next to the playground. Other facilities at this well-managed City Park include ball fields, tennis and volley ball courts.

Consider bringing a bike—there are level paved paths around the playground area that may work well for the youngest bike riders. For the more able independent rider the dirt and gravel trails at the Coot Lake location will make a more challenging outing.

Access Coot Lake recreation area from Tom Watson Park by crossing 63rd from the south end of the parking lot. You are immediately on the shoreline of this turquoise blue lake and directly in front of an accessible fishing pier. Don't expect to see people fishing at this point (at least at the weekend); this is a swimming dog's paradise and kids will love either letting their own dog swim or watch others launching off the pier in pursuit of sticks and balls. Landscaping and shoreline planting 6 years ago stabilized a chronic erosion problem. Today the area is both wildlife-rich and popular for recreation.

Fishing at Twin Lakes

Tips: At Coot Lake, bring a ball or something for your water-loving dog to retrieve. On the prairie dog trail a pair of binoculars will help you spot raptors. If your kids get completely filthy why not give them a shower at Tom Watson Park?

Away from the trailhead entrance, spread out along the 1.2 mile Lake Trail or stop at the south west end, where there is a rocky beach and picnic tables in a copse of white poplar. Continuing around Coot Lake on the north, south and west edges of the wetland, look for an unusual series of wildlife information signs. Local artist, Sue Wise, has added distinctive illustrations along with sayings and interpretations of authors and poets, to inspire visitors to reflect on the natural environment that surrounds them.

As an alternative to the Lake Loop Trail, follow the Nature Trail (accessed via the maintenance track on the south of Coot Lake) for sightings of prairie dogs in their true prairie home rather than as residents of urban sidewalks. The new prairie dog interpretative trail provides some of the best wildlife information signs in the Front Range; look at the large photos of wildlife you might expect to see and don't miss the oversize panel titled "A house in a town..." that shows inside a prairie dog burrow with all its different chambers. Watch for occasional glimpses of hunting raptors; this area is also designated as critical wildlife habitat and supports many different birds of prey. If possible, walk or cycle this trail early in the morning when wildlife is more active.

See prairie dogs in their true prairie setting

Other options:

1. Bike to Coot Lake/Tom Watson Park. 63rd Street has designated bike lanes and is a popular cycle route. This route can be connected from the Twin Lakes and Cottontail/Homestead multiuse trails in Gunbarrel, or from the bike trails in North Boulder.

2. North Boulder Reservoir Bike Loop. For those riders with child seat carriers or bike trailers, it's possible to ride through to North Boulder Reservoir (there is no entrance fee from this direction). A loop to the north combines multiuse trails and some quiet on-street biking on 55th, then 51st and then back south of the Boulder Reservoir entrance and across the dam making an approximately six mile round trip.

3. Eaton Park and Twin Lakes. Continue the natural theme by visiting Eaton Park with its grassland and wetlands, or Twin Lakes from the same parking area. This location is tucked away down a no outlet road. Come here for a peaceful getaway from Boulder's busier parks. From Diagonal Highway, drive south on 63rd Street for 0.7 miles. Turn left onto Nautilus Drive. At the two-way junction, turn left (north) and follow Nautilus Drive to its end (total: 1.1 miles). Park in the circular area. **Eaton Park** is on the north side of the road. Look for the shelter and picnic table with grassland and wetland to the north. Don't miss the mini dirt BMX bike track just north of the shelter in a small depression. Any confident 4 or 5 year old independent biker will have a blast going up and down some of the easier dirt mounds (don't visit after rain when the mud is thick and sticky). Follow the gentle trails through the park—bike and stroller accessible. Look for the new interpretative signs describing 'dry wetland' i.e. wetlands that are not visibly wet and what wildlife they attract. **Twin Lakes** is accessed on the south side of the road. Gravel trails loop round the two shaded lakes with an easily accessible irrigation ditch separating the two. Either cycle the loops, try some fishing, look for birdlife or simply see how fast leaves, sticks but hopefully not your toes move in the ditch stream. See Boulder County Parks and Open Space for more information: www.co.boulder.co.us/openspace.

4. Haystack Mountain Goat Dairy. It's hard to find places where children can get close to farm animals but this is one of them. Tour the goat farm, let the kids play with the (goat) kids, and taste the latest of their award-winning cheeses. Visit the Goat Dairy on free drop-in days, Tuesday and Saturday between noon and 2pm (year-round) when the farm is open to the public. The farm is located at 5239 Niwot Road, just north of Coot Lake near the 63rd Street/Niwot Rd intersection. For more information: 303 530 3777 web:www:haystackgoatcheese.com. Note: The dairy is moving to a new location on Oxford and 63rd in 2008.

7 CROWN ROCK

Check out the haunt of boulderers and rock climbers. Weave your way between all sorts of crazy shaped boulders. Find nooks, crannies and mini caves. Help your child scramble up something easy and fun. Enjoy the quiet of the pine-covered slopes and take in great views of the First Flatiron and the eastern plains.

Crown Rock Area—Flagstaff Mountain

Flagstaff Road, Boulder 80302
City of Boulder Mountain Parks and Open Space
303 441 3440
www.bouldercolorado.gov

Location: 3.1 miles from Broadway and Baseline Road.

Directions: From the Broadway and Baseline Road intersection drive west on Baseline for 1.4 miles. The road turns sharply right and starts to climb up what is now Flagstaff Road. Follow this steeply round tight bends for a further 1.7 miles to reach a small roadside parking area on the left. This location is referred to as Crown Rock on Open Space maps and as Flagstaff to climbers.

Parking: There are 8 designated vehicle spaces at Crown Rock. For additional parking drive a further 50 yards to 8-10 spaces on the north (right) side. Note this location is a Fee Permit area. However, if your vehicle was registered in Boulder County there is no charge. Otherwise there is a $3 parking fee. Get an envelope at the fee station by the parking and don't forget. This policy is enforced and they ticket!

Season: Good shade and breezes on a hot day. Avoid high wind days. The Great Ridge area has south-facing walls and can be nicely warm on a sunny winter day.

Restrooms: No. Note a vault restroom is due to be installed next to the parking lot in 2006. Restrooms are available at other stopping points on Flagstaff Road; see the Crown Rock orientation board at the parking lot.

Water: No.

Dogs: Yes. On-leash.

Few kids can resist weird looking rocks and large boulders. You just never know what's around the corner. This location is all about exploration, scrambling over things and finding 'secret' nooks. It also has picnic tables and some well-marked trails. We recommend this area more for the 2-5 years than the active crawlers and just walking—the ground can be uneven, slippery and prickly for soft hands.

Although you'll come across a few picnickers and tourists, this location is most visited by climbers. Flagstaff is nationally renowned for its hundreds of coarse red sandstone boulders. This is where you come to practice sequences of moves (known as 'problems') and develop climbing strength and technique. Each problem has its own name and a difficulty grade. Bouldering is a distinct style of climbing, an art in its own right, and loved and practiced exclusively by many. Flagstaff has played a prominent role in American climbing history, as the place where cutting edge problems were developed by leading climbers of the day. Today you will find many ages and abilities using this area including family

Crown Rock Area, South Side

groups. Don't be put off by the intent persistence of some of these boulderers as they repeatedly try the same boulder problem jumping onto their large squashy pads; they are usually a pretty friendly crowd and glad to see kids having as much fun as themselves in their favorite location.

There are two areas to explore at Flagstaff. The Crown Rock area is on the south side of Flagstaff road, and provides closest access. Step onto the trail from the parking lot and head up towards the picnic tables and some mini scrambles to get the views towards Denver. Alternatively follow a quarter mile mini loop trail, at times steeply up and down, which gives access to most of the big boulders and brings you back to where you started.

For a quieter, away from the road experience, go to the Upper Crown Rock area on the opposite side of the road. Here you will see the prominent Flagstaff Mountain Trail. Hike this for 50 yards until you come the sign for Upper Crown Rock and right branching trail. Follow this and you will enter big boulder country. If you want to explore more areas, or this area is simply too busy with climbers,

The boulder house - a perfect prize for reaching the Great Ridge area.

Tips: Make sure your child has shoes with a good grip for scrambling over rocks. If the parents in the group are climbers, the kids will love to join in with a chalk bag, toothbrush and playing around the crash pad even if they don't want to climb on the rock! Bring food and water.

retrace your steps to the main trail. Follow this uphill for another 250 yards (two and half zigzags) to where another small trail branches to the right. This trail gives access to a fin-like ridge of rock known as 'The Great Ridge' extending northwards up the hill. Peek through the gaps in the ridge for views and cooling breezes but hang on to your child! The prize for those that make it to this area is the mini 'boulder house"—a slab of rock balanced horizontally over three boulders. It's a perfect under 5's size and has three entrance/exits. If you fail to find it, look for the big rock at the end of the ridge with a metal pole sticking out of it (it's actually a lightening conductor), and then come south along the ridge for 30 yards. By now you've probably had quite enough of playing dens, spaceships or monster planets. Head for home.

Other options:

1. Flagstaff Mountain and Nature Center. Check out summit views of the Continental Divide, a great choice of trails and picnic areas and Flagstaff Nature Center. The log cabin Center has many hands-on exhibits staffed by friendly and knowledgeable volunteers. Open from 10:30am-4pm on Saturdays and Sundays, May through September. Also try the sensory trail at Artist's Point where you follow a rope, and with eyes closed, try to identify what you feel. Restrooms are available. Directions: Continue up Flagstaff road for a further 1.3 miles, and then turn right on Flagstaff Summit Road for 0.5 miles (vehicle access from May to October only). For more information on education and visitor programs for kids see www.bouldercolorado.gov and search on Flagstaff Nature Center.

2. Gregory Canyon. Continue the rocks and canyons theme by visiting Gregory Canyon located at the start of Flagstaff Road, 1.4 miles from Broadway. For a canyon hike, take the 0.4 mile Amphitheatre Trail which crosses a bridge and then goes up the draw steeply past Gregory amphitheatre, a little bay in the rocks where you often see climbers. Pause and explore this area. This hike will best suit your more able hiker. Parking can be difficult on weekends. See: www.bouldercolorado.gov

3. Visit Chautauqua Park. For hiking, picnicking, playgrounds and the City of Boulder Ranger Cottage located at the base of Flagstaff Road, 1 mile from Broadway (pg 34).

8 CU CAMPUS

Immerse your children in 'Discovery Corner' at CU Natural History Museum where kids are invited to touch, feel and pick up everything! Choose from doing your own animal puppet show in a tree house, to exploring themed boxes all about beavers, bats and even bison. Afterwards spread out on the CU campus whether it's along the bridges, streams and ponds of the Norlin Quadrangle, in the perfect stone amphitheater behind the Museum, or playing hide and seek near the maze-like Engineering building.

CU Natural History Museum and Campus

Henderson Building UCB218, Boulder 80309
University of Colorado
303 492 6892
www.cumuseum.colorado.edu

Open Hours: Museum: Monday to Friday 9am-5pm, Saturday 9am-4pm, Sunday 10am-4pm. Free entrance.

Location: Just east of Broadway, between 15th and 16th Streets on CU Campus.

Public Transportation: RTD/SKIP buses stop at 16th/Euclid and Broadway.

Directions: The CU Natural History Museum is located in Henderson Building between 15th and 16th Streets on CU Campus. CU campus extends along Broadway from University Avenue to Baseline, and stretches eastwards to 28th Street.

Parking: Possibly the best way to get to the Museum and CU campus is by bike, foot or bus. Failing this, there is parking in residential streets west of Broadway; these can be very busy and there is a two hour limit during weekdays. On CU Campus, the parking lot in front of the Museum is available during weekends for a flat rate fee (currently $2). This lot can only be entered driving north on Broadway; take the first sharp right (looks improbable) after Euclid across the bike path and through the barrier entrance. For weekday visitors, CU parking is located in the Euclid parking structure where it is $1.50/hour from 9am-5pm and then a flat rate (currently $2) after 5pm and at weekends.

Season: All year. Good fall color from the large trees on campus.

Restrooms: Fully equipped restrooms with wheelchair access in the Natural History Museum.

Water: Drinking fountains on 1st and 3rd floors of the Natural History Museum.

Dogs: No dogs inside the Natural History Museum. On-leash on campus.

CU Campus, a glorious sandstone maze of tall buildings and secret alleyways, spreads over seemingly half of central Boulder. Crowds of students, a myriad of paths, and difficult parking keeps this location off the radar screen for most parents. However, take the time to explore the Campus and you'll be rewarded with some great activities for the under 5's as well as exposing young minds to the great halls of learning and their environs!

The CU Natural History Museum provides one of the best free education resources in Boulder. With over 4 million specimens, you can bet there'll be something of interest. The Henderson building lies just off Broadway. Enter through the double black doors either at the front or with a ramp at the back

Skip on the Shakespeare Stage

(east entrance). Recent facelifts include the Dinosaur Hall, and the addition of a children's 'Discovery Corner'. Themed animal boxes in the Discovery area contain all sorts of things to touch from bones, pelts and photographs, to fact sheets and storybooks. The adjacent ground floor display of birds and animals are great for picking out a particular bird or animal you've seen in your yard. Look for the free "Family Days" held about 3 times a year, where the museum provides hands-on learning activities on all floors with a special focus on their latest exhibits. There is no entrance fee for the Museum, but to help with running costs a voluntary fee of $3 is suggested for adults.

Check the museum website before visiting for latest information.

Outside the Henderson building's east doors, kids may enjoy the stage and steps of the secluded sandstone amphitheatre, where the annual Shakespeare Festival is held. Walking north and turning immediately right, you will come to the Shakespeare Gardens—raised beds at the far east end of the School of Education courtyard—containing the herbs, flowers and vegetables mentioned in the plays with the relevant quotations on signs. If you continue walking northwards from the amphitheater, you come to the open grassy area of the Norlin Quadrangle—a surprisingly large amount of green and open space on the Campus. Landscaped streams, bridges, picnic areas and tall shade trees make this a fun place to explore ending in a large pond near University Avenue. Look for lazily swimming bright orange Koi carp and possibly a glimpse of basking turtles. This area will be busy during term time—see Tips for visiting during recess.

Tips: To avoid Campus crowds, visit at a weekend or during school breaks; summer recess is May through August. Bring a stroller; the CU Campus can get very large with a toddler. Check the CU Natural History Museum website before you visit for detailed information on directions, parking and latest exhibit information at: www.cumuseum.colorado.edu

Other options:

1. Fiske Planetarium and Science Center. The Planetarium is located south of the Henderson Building on Regent Drive—look for the white geodesic dome. In the entrance lobby there is open access to exhibits where you can split light into rainbows and touch a meteorite. There are also regular family shows such as "Kids in Space' and 'Adventures beyond the Solar System' which are targeted at kids 4 years old and up for which there is a $3.50 charge. For more information see www.cosmos.colorado.edu/sbo or call 303 492 5002.

2. Colorado Scale Model Solar System. This is a self-guided walk that starts in front of Fiske Planetarium and goes north across the campus. The model planets represent the vastness of the solar system on a scale of one to ten billion. The model is dedicated to the crew of the Challenger mission including Ellison S. Onizuka who was a CU alumnus.

3. Extra Campus Stuff. Check out the CU bouldering walls on the Engineering building located on the east side of Campus, just west of Regent Drive. A strange light catching mosaic and striking sculptures mark the entrance to a maze of walls and ledges with climbable edges. Great for shaded play and exploring round corners. It is also a popular site for serious climbers to get strong traversing the stone walls. Free parking is available on weekends at the nearby large lot on the corner of Regent Drive and Colorado Avenue, next to 28th Street.

4. University Hill Elementary School—16th and Euclid Avenue. Located on the opposite side of Broadway from the CU museum, University Hill Elementary School has large grounds with 3 different playground areas stretching westwards. There are a range of swings and play structures, some in the shade and sheltered. When school is not in session there is public access to the grounds.

EAST BOULDER COMMUNITY CENTER 9

Look into the jaws of a dinosaur at this imaginatively themed playground at East Boulder Community Center. Let your dog run off leash and take a dip in the small lake at the adjacent City Dog Park. Explore the pond near the Center, then bike or hike a short distance to South Boulder Creek and find a great area for tree climbing and getting down to the stream. Make a hike of it and take a half mile round trip along the Creek to another small playground.

East Boulder Community Center and South Boulder Creek Trail

5660 Sioux Drive, Boulder 80303
For Community Center information:
City of Boulder Parks and Recreation
303 441 4400
www.bouldercolorado.gov
City of Boulder Open Space and Mountain Parks
303 441 3440
www.bouldercolorado.gov

Location: 2.1 miles from Broadway and Table Mesa Drive.

Public Transportation: RTD services 203 and 206 stop outside the Community Center.

Directions: From the intersection with Broadway, follow Table Mesa Drive east for 1.4 miles over US36 (Table Mesa Drive is now called South Boulder Road). Turn left onto 55th which is also signposted East Boulder Community Center. Follow 55th as it turns into Sioux Drive which goes round the east side of the Community Center. It ends at a STOP sign where you turn left into the parking lot.

Parking: Large paved parking lot with space for over 100 vehicles. Park at the west end for closest access to the playground.

Season: All year. Large cottonwoods on the South Boulder Creek Trail provide shade in the summer and great fall color.

Restrooms: Fully equipped restrooms with wheelchair access available when the Community Center is open; the west entrance side door is nearest to the playground. The Center's open hours change for the summer and winter season, but generally follow daylight patterns. See the website for details.

Water: Drinking fountains by the restrooms inside the Community Center.

Dogs: Yes on the South Boulder Creek Trail, on-leash or City of Boulder voice and sight control standard. All other areas on-leash—but see Dog Park. No dogs allowed in the playground.

A trip to East Boulder Community Center provides a nicely contrasting outing. Choose between the dinosaur playground and the looped paths around the Recreation Center, or branch off onto the South Boulder Creek Trail for woodlands and streamside exploration.

The Community Center is scenically located down a dead end road surrounded by ponds, open grassland and bordered by tall cottonwoods to the east along the South Boulder Creek Trail. The large parking lot provides easy access both to the outdoor grounds of the Community Center as well as the popular South Boulder Creek Trail.

Tips: Look for the distinctive red tail of the Red-tailed Hawks which nest in nearby cottonwoods and are actively circling in the sky and calling in the spring/summer months. The South Boulder Creek Trail can be busy with bikes, runners, horse riders and dog walkers year-round. For a quieter experience visit this area mid-week or at off-peak weekend times.

The playground is located to the west of the Community Center and has a dinosaur theme. Put your hand in the mouth of the largest one! Facilities include 2 large ramp and slide structures, child and tot swings, boulders with dinosaurs painted on them, picnic tables and 2 shelters. The playground is fenced and reached by paved paths from the parking lot. These paths also loop round the Community Center and its large pond, providing some good riding for able as well as just-starting bike riders. Facilities inside the Community Center include food and drink machines. As you approach the entrance note the xeriscape demonstration planting and Garden in a Box project.

To reach the South Boulder Creek Trail, follow a paved path east from the parking lot (past a small pond used by duck and geese) looking for signs marking the trail. Cross the wooden bridge and reach the trail proper running in a north/south direction. This section of the Creek Trail between Baseline Road and South Boulder Road is known as the Bobolink Trail and is highlighted by self-guided interpretive displays themed on the riparian area. If you take the right fork of the trail you arrive within 100

Other options:

1. East Boulder Dog Park. Let your dog run off leash with access to a small lake. This popular dog park is located just south west of the playground and offers two fenced areas over a total of 0.5 acres.

2. Leisure Center Picks. Check out the climbing and bouldering wall inside the Community Center. Instruction and drop-in supervised belay sessions are provided, while bouldering to the 10 foot mark can be carried out during Center hours. The swimming pool area includes a leisure pool with lazy river, bubble bench and 150 ft. water slide.

3. South Boulder Creek Trail Links by Bike. To the North: South Boulder Creek Trail links to Boulder Creek Path at 55th. 2.6 miles distance with 1.9 miles off-street. To the South: Link to Marshall Road near Hwy93. The entire stretch of this trail is 2.8 miles off-street through largely open prairie with great views of the Rocky Mountain foothills. Note: Dogs are not allowed on the South Boulder Creek Trail south of South Boulder Road to Marshall Road.

---

yards at some large cottonwoods with streamside access. This is a great area to explore with kids with fallen trees, pebble banks and pools of water. In general, access to much of South Boulder Creek is not allowed to protect riparian wildlife, but this small area allows exploration in a beautiful setting. If you cross the Creek to the west and follow a small dirt trail southwards through grass and woodland, this will link to a small log playground with swings backing onto the creek at the end of Ontario Place. There and back will make a short trip of about half a mile from the Community Center; you can be sure there will be no crowds at this smaller play area.

Look for displays by the striking pale-helmeted Bobolink (for which this trail was named) and other ground nesting birds in the fields to the east, from mid-May through the summer. White-tailed and mule deer are common, and foxes and coyotes sometimes sighted. At the south end of the creek trail the historic Van Vleet Ranch has fields grazed by livestock and two historic barn structures, Dorn Barn and Abernathy Barn which are over 100 years old. Look for new-born calves in the spring!

10 EBEN G. FINE PARK

Escape the heat and wade, play, or picnic right next to Boulder Creek under large shade trees. Tucked at the entrance to Boulder Canyon, little 'Eben G.' offers a brand new playground and easy access to the creek, with plenty of picnic and barbeque sites. Follow the creek-side trail west of the pedestrian underpass in a wilder setting to the kayak and tubing put-in location at Matt's Whitewater Park.

Eben G. Fine Park and Matt's Whitewater Park

4th and Arapahoe, Boulder 80302
City of Boulder Parks and Recreation
303 413 7200
www.bouldercolorado.gov

Location: 0.8 miles from Broadway and Arapahoe Avenue.

Public Transportation: RTD buses stop on Arapahoe Avenue, a short distance from the park.

Directions: From Broadway drive west on Arapahoe Avenue for 0.8 miles to the sign for the park on the right. Take an immediate right at the mini roundabout and follow a paved road for 50 yards down to the parking lot.

Parking: Paved parking lot with space for about 20 vehicles. Additional parking is located further west along Arapahoe Avenue on the south side of the park; go straight ahead from the mini roundabout for 0.1 miles to reach parking on the right.

Season: All year. Especially good for shade and cooling canyon breezes in summer. Loses sun early in winter.

Restrooms: Fully equipped restrooms with wheelchair access available in a stone building near the playground (summer only). In winter a port-a-potty restroom with wheelchair access is available in the first parking lot described.

Water: Drinking fountain located between the playground and the group shelter (summer only).

Dogs: Yes. On-leash.

Hidden at the entrance to Boulder Canyon, and just across the Creek from Settlers Park, Eben G. offers a respite from summer heat with plenty of shade from large maple trees (including over the playground) and easy access to the river. The park is named after Eben G. Fine, discoverer of Arapahoe Glacier, which supplies much of Boulder's drinking water.

This park can be popular on hot weekends because of its location right next to Boulder Creek. On such days, settle back to watch the spectacle of people floating down on inner tubes or bring your own child-sized version to play with in shallow pools at the creek edge.

At other times of the week and in different seasons the park provides a quiet location with good picnic and play facilities. Expect some noise from adjacent highway traffic going up Boulder Canyon,

but this is drowned out by high volume creek flows in May/June.

    The smart new playground area includes a boulder and sand area for digging, a typical slide structure with mini climbing panel and natural-look rock wall plus 4 child and 2 tot swings. This area is fenced on one side to prevent tots running out onto the adjacent path and creek. Next to the playground a large group shelter contains picnic tables in addition to those located under trees next to the creek.

    Boulder Creek Trail passes through the park at its east end by the parking lot. This paved multiuse trail can be very busy with different users, but is set away from the playground and creek. At the west end of the park a branch of the Creek Trail leads nothwest to Settlers Park

Matt's Whitewater Park

Tips: Walk or bike to the park on a hot summer weekend and avoid vehicle parking hassles; otherwise park early before the tubers arrive. Bring sand and water toys for the creek and playground. Look for the grey American Dipper bobbing on creek boulders and sticking its head under water.

Other options:

1. Matt's Whitewater Park. To enjoy the creek in a wilder woodland setting, follow the Boulder Creek Trail west for an additional 5-10mins walk. A short but steep gravel bank descends by the sign. Watch the kayakers and tubers, then make a round trip by following the dirt creek-side trail east back to Eben G.

2. Boulder Canyon - History Interpretative Trail. For information on the history of Boulder Canyon and Creek look for small brown interpretative signs located along the paved Creek Trail from Eben G. westwards. See historic photos; learn about water supply and spot remnants of the old water ditch above the current flowing Farm Ditch.

3. Settlers Park. Walk or bike 0.1 miles to Settlers Park to explore the red fins of rock that can be easily seen from Eben G. To get there take the underpass and paved trail at the west end of the park (5-10mins pg 52).

4. Boulder Creek Trail—Bike Links West and East. Follow the Boulder Creek Trail west, at first on a paved track, to reach an area known as Elephant Rock, popular with rock climbers. The trail climbs steadily (now on gravel and not recommended for road bikes) and criss-crosses the creek to reach its end after 2.3 miles. Follow the Boulder Creek Trail east for one mile to reach downtown Boulder and City Park. This part of the trail passes the Evert Pierson Kid's Fishing Ponds and then the Charles A. Haertling Sculpture Garden (pg 30).

ELDORADO CANYON 11

Eldorado Canyon State Park

Eldorado Springs, CO 80025
Colorado State Parks
303 494 3943
www.parks.state.co.us

Open Hours: State Park: Sunrise to sunset year round. Visitor Center: 9am-5pm daily. Vehicle entrance fee $5/car unless you have a State Park annual pass.
Location: 3.2 miles from Broadway and Eldorado Springs Drive (Hwy170).
Directions: From the intersection of Broadway and Hwy170, drive west on Hwy170 (also signed as Eldorado Springs Drive). This will bring you to the entrance of Eldorado Springs. Continue on the pot-holed road for a further 0.4 miles to the State Park entrance.
Parking: There are two main parking areas in the Park; one immediately after the entrance, and the other by the Visitor Center reached by driving 1 mile up the dirt road. Both parking lots have a gravel surface and space for approximately 80 cars.
Season: Attractive in all seasons. However Eldorado Canyon can be cold; it acts as a wind funnel in the spring, and loses the sun early in winter.
Restrooms: 2 vault restrooms at the lower parking lot and 2 vault restrooms at the upper parking lot on the south side of South Boulder Creek. In addition fully equipped restrooms inside the Visitor Center are available during open hours. All restrooms have wheelchair access.
Water: Drinking fountains are located by the restrooms inside the Visitor Center. No water outside.
Dogs: Yes. On-leash.

Plenty to see and do at this rock climber's paradise. Be dwarfed by towering red sandstone walls, hundreds of feet high. Watch the antics of climbers, or join in if you know how. Scramble around large boulders, splash in the creek, try some fishing, hike a trail with push button signs, or picnic with shade and cool breezes on a hot summer's day. Plan to stay a while.

For over 100 years, people have been flocking to Eldorado Springs to marvel at the 1000 foot vertical walls and spend some time in this impressive canyon. Between 1904 and 1928, a successful resort operated at the canyon's mouth drawing visitors from Denver and beyond with the lure of warm Artesian Springs. Today Eldorado Canyon State Park is a day use area attracting thousands of people to bike, hike, picnic, fish, and especially to rock climb within the canyon's walls.

For the under 5's this is a great place to explore rocks and boulders, oggle at climbers, explore a short trail, or simply picnic and splash in South Boulder Creek.

At the entrance booth pick up a brochure and orient yourself.

Streamside Trail, Lower Area Choose the lower parking lot as a base for a more active outing. Opt for the 0.5 mile Streamside Trail and follow a narrow path past small caves and over and under huge boulders. The first 300 feet are stroller and wheelchair accessible. From here on scramble along the twisting trail, at times close to the creek. If your kids are curious about climbing, this is THE trail in the park to see climbing up close. On the south side of the bridge, climbers will literally start where the cliff meets the road, making sure to keep their ropes out of the way of cars! On the north side of

the creek, look for tiny figures linked by ropes hundreds of feet up the cliff. In the climbing world, Eldorado Canyon is internationally known for its hundreds of quality climbs on the sheer canyon walls; attested to by the fact that over 75% of its annual visitors are there to climb. In spring the normally quiet creek roars into action with snowmelt runoff surging beneath the bridge. Enjoy the drama, but watch your kids!

Streamside Trail, Upper Area For a more laid back visit, drive one mile up the canyon road to the upper parking area next to the Visitor Center. Over 40 picnic and barbeque sites are spread out on both sides of the creek with lots of shade, and easy creek-side access. Appreciate mid-summer temperatures that at times can be 15 degrees lower than on the Denver plains. Many people know this, so expect large groups of all nationalities enjoying a day out with barbeques in full swing.

If you are looking for an activity consider the following:

Fishing The cold creek waters are home to rainbow and brown trout. If you are under 16, no fishing permit is required. Pick up a brochure for more information at the Visitor Center.

Wading This is the best area in the Park to go wading. Generally the water flows shallowly and gently and kids are forever building stone dams. Note that during Mid-May to Mid-June spring run off can make the Creek too rough for entry. The creek floor has sharp stones; bring swim shoes or equivalent.

Climbing and Scrambling If your kids like scrambling around large boulders, there are plenty of opportunities in this upper area. Near the wooden bridge on the north side of the road, there is a giant block set back amongst the trees. Play hide and seek around this and the clusters of pine trees and try

Tips: Arrive early on a summer weekend. Once the State Park reaches vehicle capacity they start turning cars away, sometimes by 10am! Bring binoculars (to watch the climbers and the birds), swim shoes (for wading) in the creek, and plenty of water. Climbers, bring a top rope if you want to let your kids climb at Supremacy Slabs. Especially important, pack an all-frills picnic—or the grilling parties in the upper parking lot will have your mouth watering insanely all day long.

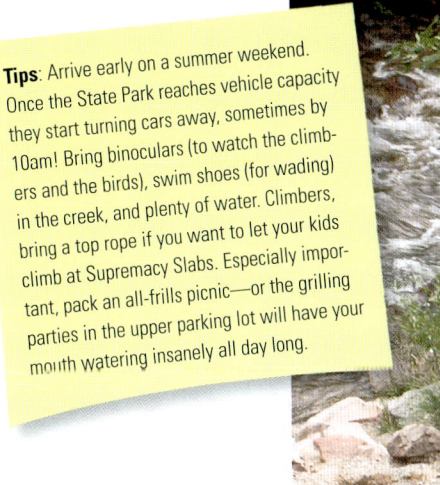

This page: Climbing at Supremacy Slabs - Upper area. Opposite page: Explore the cave on the Streamside Trail.

scrambling over smaller nearby rocks. You may also see climbers trying hard boulder problems on this same lump of rock. Don't walk underneath them and risk getting squashed!

If you climb and want to let your kids try some rock-climbing, set up a top rope at the popular Supremacy Slabs located immediately south of the bridge. The easy angled slabs and convenient trees for setting up top ropes make this a popular teaching site.

Nature Trail If you want to hike on easy ground with a stroller, do the first half of the 0.7 mile Fowler Trail. A series of 'watchable' wildlife interpretative signs can be found along it which includes buttons to press and things to touch. Although the trail is flat, the canyon drops away to its south side giving great views of the rock walls and another chance to watch rock climbers (although this time from a distance). Bring binoculars to look at birds, climbers and cliffs. Look for Prairie Falcons soaring around; they nest high up in the canyon walls and sometimes dive bomb a pigeon for breakfast!

Visitor Center Packed with information and books, the Visitor Center also has a board with monthly listings of nature events and sightings. There are two displays on the wall; one on the history of climbing and the other on the history of Eldorado Springs. Look at the photos on the latter and be amazed by the pictures of tightrope walker, Ivy Baldwin, crossing between the sandstone towers at Eldorado Canyon's entrance nearly 100 years ago. Baldwin performed this feat for tourists 89 times up to 1928. Typically a crossing would take 6.5 minutes, during which he would stand on his head on the tensioned cable, 400 foot off the ground. His last crossing was at the age of 81!

Other options:

1. Artesian Springs Resort. Get a taste of Eldorado's past at the old Artesian Springs resort. The outdoor swimming pool is located 0.3 miles west of the Eldorado Springs entrance, on the same road as the State Park. The water should be warm; it's Rocky Mountain water that has reached a depth of 8,000 feet underground before being forced to the surface as an Artesian Spring.

2. Doudy Draw Trail. Located 1.8 miles west of Hwy93 on Eldorado Springs Drive. Always a popular trail. Follow a small stream southwards to the former Doudy Homestead site (0.3 miles). Facilities include picnic tables and vault restrooms. The small building to the northeast of the picnic area served as a milk house; the stream was diverted to enter the milk house and keep the canisters of fresh milk cold until they could be hauled to market. The entire Doudy Draw Trail stretches 3.3 miles onto a grassland savannah before ending at the Flatirons Vista Trailhead on Hwy93. Alternatively follow the Community Ditch Trail eastwards for 1.7 miles to link in with the Marshall Mesa Trailhead on the east side of Hwy93. Arrive early before the parking lot fills on weekends. For more information see: www.bouldercolorado.gov under 'Trails'.

3. South Trailhead, Mesa Trail. This popular parking lot located opposite Doudy Draw trailhead on the north side of Eldorado Springs Drive provides numerous trail links, historic cabins and hiking options in a wildlife rich area. Vault restrooms and picnic tables are located next to the parking lot. Links to other City of Boulder trails to the north include Shadow Canyon Trail, South Boulder and Bear Peaks, or further north again to NCAR (National Center for Atmospheric Research) and six miles to Chautauqua Park. The Mesa Trail also connects to the Towhee Trail, Homestead Trail, South Boulder Creek Trail and Big Bluestem Trail. For more information see: www.bouldercolorado.gov under 'Trails'.

FOOTHILLS COMMUNITY PARK 12

This is Boulder's new showpiece—a large spectacularly located, state-of-the-art regional park due to open as this book goes to print. Choose from a climbing wall, futuristic jungle gym, swings galore, and a bi-level, very large ramp and slide structure. Also check out the new Dog Park, the community gardens, a large stand alone climbing boulder, a smaller tot friendly playground just to the south and miles of multi use paved and off road trails linking to nearby open space.

Foothills Community Park

800 Cherry Avenue, Boulder 80304
Boulder Parks and Recreation
303 413 7200
www.bouldercolorado.gov

Location: 0.3 miles from Broadway and Violet.

Public Transportation: RTD/SKIP bus services stop on Broadway and Violet.

Directions: From the Broadway intersection drive west on Violet Avenue. Turn right onto 10th and then left onto Cherry Avenue. Use the parking lot on the south side of the road or continue to the end of Cherry Avenue and turn right onto 7th, where the second large parking lot is located.

Parking: The Cherry Avenue paved parking lot is located next to the Community Gardens and provides space for up to 100 vehicles and closest access to the smaller south playground. The 7th Avenue paved parking lot is located next to the large playground and provides space for up to 100 cars. This is the best location to access the Dog Park.

Season: All year. This is an exposed location with little shade other than at the shelters next to the playgrounds. Avoid high wind days; in time, new planting at the large playground will provide some cover.

Restrooms: Fully equipped restrooms with wheelchair access are located near both playground areas (at the west end of the Cherry Avenue parking and at the 7th Avenue parking). Open year round.

Water: Drinking fountains located at the large playground on 7th and next to the smaller south playground (summer only). It is possible to obtain water from inside the restrooms year round.

Dogs: Yes. On-leash. In the Dog Park they may run off-leash in the two enclosed areas.

Billed as Boulder's first regional park this beautifully located facility with a Flatirons and Foothills open space backdrop, is being constructed over 3 phases, with the second phase of the large playground site complete as this book goes to print. Spanning several acres, the mix of informal and formal recreation areas is well served by connecting multiuse bike paths on combinations of paved and unpaved trails. Plan to spread out over a visit and bring bikes and trikes for young bikers to travel between the different areas using the smooth level paths and connecting loops.

The south part of Foothills Community Park consists of the Cherry Avenue parking lot, the community gardens, the smaller playground, inline hockey arenas, drinking fountains and restrooms. Facilities at the south playground include a large ramp and slide structure, 2 child and 2 infant swings, and a tots area with tall grass bordered paths, a small house and a few touch and move panels. The new

Tips: Sunscreen and hats a must in summer. Pick a non-windy day. Check out the freestanding artificial boulder by the inline hockey arenas - there's a hard way up for all members of the family. Bring bikes and trikes for easy loops and linking playgrounds.

South playground near the community gardens

community gardens site has metal sculpted vegetables on its fence, and as you pass through provides a chance to spot different vegetables. Near the hockey arena, look for a stand alone large boulder to climb on and a modernist metal peek a boo structure to its side.

The new Foothills playground is located to the north of 7th Avenue—look for sandstone entrance signs. Attention to detail includes colorful sculptures on the playground walls, and bold designs embedded in the entrance paths. The playground consists of a climbing wall, a very large bi-level ramp and slide structure, 2 tire swings and several child swings as well as the new jungle gym. 4 large shelters provide shade and accommodate picnic tables. To the north of the playground, paved trails lead to the Dog Park. Phase III development of Foothills Community Park remains several years off and includes short turf areas and ball fields to its north end.

On the wilder side, the playgrounds are surrounded by grassland where you can look for wildflowers, birds and insects. On weekends watch the paragliders descend to the ground and then fold their 'chutes'.

Other options:

1. Trailhead Links North and South. Link to multi-use trailheads on either side of Foothills Community Park; bike seat carrier/and trailer bike or jogging stroller combinations advised. South—join with Wonderland Lake via a 0.3 mile dirt trail (pg 93). North—link with Fourmile Creek Trailhead and Lee Hill Drive just past the Dog Park. East—follow paved trails to Yarmouth Avenue where a local community initiative has led to the installation of a new playground called Holiday Park.

2. Shining Mountain Waldorf School Playground. If it's just too hot or exposed at the Foothills playgrounds, retrace your steps to the Cherry Avenue parking lot. Looking eastwards over grassland you see a tempting range of wooden play structures from tree houses to tunnels and ramps. This is the play equipment of Shining Mountain Waldorf School. It is shaded, sheltered and tucked away and when school is not in session there is open access.

13 GOOSE CREEK

Climb, nature watch, rock hop and swing all at one location. Cycle as little or as far as you want along Goose Creek Trail and make eye contact with prairie dogs as you cycle through one of the largest urban dog towns in Boulder. Afterwards wear your self out climbing on a man-made boulder with multi colored holds, then cross over the road to a playground with a tire swing.

At the Stepping Stones.

Goose Creek Greenway Trail and Urban Dogtown

Mapleton Avenue, Boulder 80301
Boulder Parks and Recreation
303 413 7200
www.bouldercolorado.gov

Location: 1.4 miles from Broadway and Pine.

Public Transportation: RTD bus services stop on Mapleton Avenue and 28th.

Directions: From Broadway, drive east on Pine to the junction with 28th. Turn left onto 28th and then take the first right (look for the large YMCA building on the corner) onto Mapleton Avenue.

Parking: Park on Mapleton Avenue next to the East Mapleton Ball fields halfway down the street. Alternatively, for off road parking, use the parking lot on the west side of the ball fields behind the YMCA. This may be busy if a game is in progress.

Season: Avoid midday summer heat and high wind days

Restrooms: Fully-equipped restrooms are located just off the sidewalk next to East Mapleton Ball Fields' entrance. If these restrooms are locked, a friendly person at the Boulder Rock Club or YMCA may let you use their facilities.

Water: Yes. Drinking fountain outside the restrooms at East Mapleton Ball fields (summer only).

Dogs: Yes. On-leash.

Tucked away in central Boulder, the Goose Creek Greenway Trail provides a welcome respite of green, wetness and wildlife in an essentially urban area. This trail is included as a bike outing because it does not have the hoards of users seen on some of Boulder's other trails. There are also some great nature watching opportunities and it combines some fun elements such as large boulders and stepping stones right at the start. Even if you just stay in the immediate area of the Ball Fields and visit the retention pond, climbing boulder and playground it makes a fun and worthwhile trip for the under 5's.

Start at the entrance of East Mapleton Ball Fields, the giant boulder and playground should be in sight. Boulder Rock Club's free boulder is located outside their orange building on the north side of Mapleton. There is some shade from trees and the pea gravel base absorbs jumps and falls. Free unsupervised use is permitted.

When you tire of this, cross the street to the tire swing and slide structure at the new East Mapleton playground. This is a small site located just off street next to the YMCA parking entrance. It gets good midday shade from large trees.

Fish at the large pond at the end of Goose Creek Trail.

JOY MASTERS

Tips: At the retention pond near the Boulder Rock Club, hop over the steppingstones and don't get wet! In summer dip your toes and watch for minnows, basking turtles, and dragonflies. Bring a net to search for 3 inch crawdads in the Creek near the railway-bridge (this is the second underpass down the trail from the start—about 2min on a bike or 10min walk). Bring a picnic for your stop next to the large pond at the trail end junction with Boulder Creek Trail. As you watch the prairie dogs, look for the different behaviors of alarm barks, feeding, nesting (collecting vegetation in their mouths to take down the burrow), and 'kissing' greetings with their teeth.

The 1.6-mile (one way) bike trip on Goose Creek Greenway is accessed via a paved path on the north side of the street, opposite the Ball Fields. The retention pond at the start has Red-winged blackbirds and cattails, the stepping stones across the water are located around the corner to the west. For a trike and just-starting bike rider, this is a good place to pedal on smooth easy surfaces.

To cycle Goose Creek Trail we recommend bike seat carriers or trailer combinations unless you have a good independent young rider. This recommended ride stretches eastwards from just below 28th Street to just before 55th on a gentle downhill gradient. A little after the second (railway bridge) underpass, make a stop at a small waterfall pond feature with upright stones and grass.

Above: Climb the giant boulder outside the Boulder Rock Club.
Left: Catching crawdads near the railway bridge.

Other options:

1. Goose Creek Trail Loop. Make a loop of Goose Creek Trail by turning right at the Boulder Creek Trail junction and following it past the southwest corner of the pond. Go straight at the next junction paralleling Pearl Parkway. Cross over 49th at the stoplight and keep heading west, passing business parks, then under Foothills Parkway and then via Frontier Avenue until you reach 30th. Turn right and cycle north on the sidewalk until you reach Mapleton Avenue after 0.2 miles. This round trip part of the loop is not the most scenic, but it does make a 3 mile loop almost all off street, for those who dislike doubling back.

2. Ice Cream. Indulge yourselves at nearby 'Glacier Ice Cream' located in the small shopping center on the west side of 28th between Valmont and Glenwood Drive.

Go under Foothills Parkway via the under pass to reach 47th Street and cross the road. From here the trail is open as well as more urban but you have also arrived in Dog Town. Pause to make eye contact and watch the inhabitant's antics. (Note: This population will likely be relocated when Valmont City Park is developed some years ahead—but see prairie dogs in their natural habitat at Coot Lake (pg 38). At the junction with Wonderland Creek Greenway, keep right and follow the trail round under Pearl to a mini oasis among busy roads. Here Goose Creek Trail ends and becomes Boulder Creek Trail. A large retention pond and stands of cattail trap sediment from the drainage channels. Look carefully and you may see a muskrat (not to mention more prairie dogs). Continue a little further east; tall willows provide shade and exploring opportunities next to Boulder Creek. You are now located just west of 55th. Pause next to the creek, dip your toes, have a snack and then retrace your steps.

HAWTHORN GARDENS

14

This is the Mecca for all things green. Bike next to a flowing irrigation ditch and take in the scene of over 170 plots producing flowers and vegetables. Help your kids spot different vegetables as you find your way through the maze of individual gardens to the colorful Children's Garden. Pause to take in the colors, smells and food-seeking wildlife (birds, chipmunks, squirrels) and then take some ideas home for growing something of your own.

Children's Peace Garden at Hawthorn Community Gardens

16th Street and Hawthorn Avenue, Boulder 80304
Growing Gardens of Boulder County
303 413 7248
www.growinggardens.org

Location: 0.25 miles from Broadway and Iris.

Public Transportation: RTD Route 208 and SKIP buses stop on Broadway at the turn to North Boulder Recreation Center.

Directions: Drive east on Iris for 4 blocks and turn right onto 16th Street. Follow 16th to its end, then turn left (east) onto Hawthorn Avenue. The Community Gardens are to the south and accessed by the paved multiuse trail. Alternatively, start your visit from North Boulder Recreation Center at 3170 Broadway between Evergreen and Forest; follow the paved path eastwards, then turn left (north) along a multi-use bike trail for a total distance of 1/8th mile.

Parking: Park on the quiet residential streets of Hawthorn and 16th. Alternatively, North Boulder Recreation Center has a large paved parking lot. If this looks full, drive to the north end where there is usually space.

Season: All year, but visit the Community Gardens during the growing season between April and September. The site is exposed so avoid midday heat. Tall trees provide shade on the south and west sides of the site and there is a fun little shelter with vines growing up its walls located on the central track between the plots.

Restrooms: From mid-April to mid-September a port-a-potty is available at Hawthorn Community Gardens. Fully equipped restrooms are available in the Recreation Center during open hours.

Water: Bottles can be filled at the spigot. Drinking fountains outside the restrooms in North Boulder Recreation Center.

Dogs: Yes. On-leash.

If you have a fascination for growing things, then this is the place for you. And even if you don't, then the color, odd glimpse of a familiar vegetable, maze-like garden layout, running irrigation ditch and paved bike paths linking to North Boulder Recreation Center make this a good outing.

The large acreage of Hawthorn Community Gardens is the focus of the non-profit organization, Growing Gardens, which works to 'cultivate community through gardening'. Growing Gardens nurtures a large and colorful Children's Garden, an 'Able Garden' (demonstrating raised bed gardening for people with disabilities), and oversees more than 170 community garden plots available to the public. In addition there are two greenhouses used by youth and community programs to grow food for neighborhood projects, as well as windrow composting (where local residents are able to compost their garden waste in long rows) and a compost demonstration area with signs and different types of bins.

Visit this location during the growing season to encounter a hub of activity. Many gardens are managed as a family project, and kids abound digging, watering and generally getting involved. Take a route through the grid of garden plots to the far east end. As you do so, help your kids spot different plants, vegetables, insects or anything else of interest. The 'prize' at the end is the colorful Children's Garden where brightly painted pickets decorated with vegetable shapes entice you through the archway. The purpose of this garden is to teach children the source of food from seed to plate, and instill a sense of wonder at all things growing. Kids are encouraged to explore, touch and smell plants in the garden and no one will object if the odd flower is picked, or something munched on. Look for the salsa and pizza gardens and sit under the teepee!

For the adults in the group, the Community Gardens are a great place to get some ideas and demystify vegetable growing. For the construction fan, check out the array of home built structures for growing vines, vegetables and other plants vertically. Similarly look at the different types of raised garden beds.

For young bike and trike riders, the paved and level paths on the west and south sides of this site provide easy riding. The trail to the west is bordered by an irrigation ditch which flows swiftly during spring/summer months. Dip your toes and look for the dense red mats of willow roots in the banksides.

Other options:

1. Long's Iris Gardens. Visit neighboring Iris Gardens and be overwhelmed by color from 1000's of blooming bearded iris. Entrance is free during the short open season from April 30th to June 12th when the iris are in flower and plants available to the public. Walk around the 100 year old family business admiring the old buildings and farm machinery. Harness your kids' energy by letting them help you dig up an iris (instructions, bag and a shovel are provided) and then nurture these easily grown plants at home as a family project.

2. North Boulder Recreation Center. Swim at North Boulder Recreation Center's new pool, which comes with water buckets, large spiral slide, water baseball hoops and a separate super-wide tots slide. For non-swimmers the lounge observation area, located just inside the entrance has comfy chairs and makes a good air-conditioned retreat in winter or summer. See: www.bouldercolorado.gov. 303 413 7260.

3. 'Food is from Venus, Farming is from Mars'. Let your 5 yr old learn about the source of the food they eat in a fun 4-week course at the Children's Peace garden. See www.growinggardens.org for more information.

4. Eats and Treats Broadway Community Plaza. Walk or bike four blocks south on 13th Street, a quiet residential street, to reach Broadway Community Plaza where good things to eat abound (pg 81).

Tips: For 'vegetable spotting' at the Community Gardens visit between late June and early September when tomatoes, beans, squash and other produce will be most obvious to kids and when the site is at its most colorful. Play a gentle hide and seek around the garden plots and when you stop, check out what vegetables you can see.

MISSION

Growing Gardens' mission is to enrich the lives of Boulder County residents through environmentally sustainable gardening programs that empower people to experience a direct and deep connection with plants, the land and each other.

Our goals are: Empowerment, Education, Facilitation, Fostering Community and Environmental Protection.

Please visit our website to learn more about our programs.

www.growinggardens.org

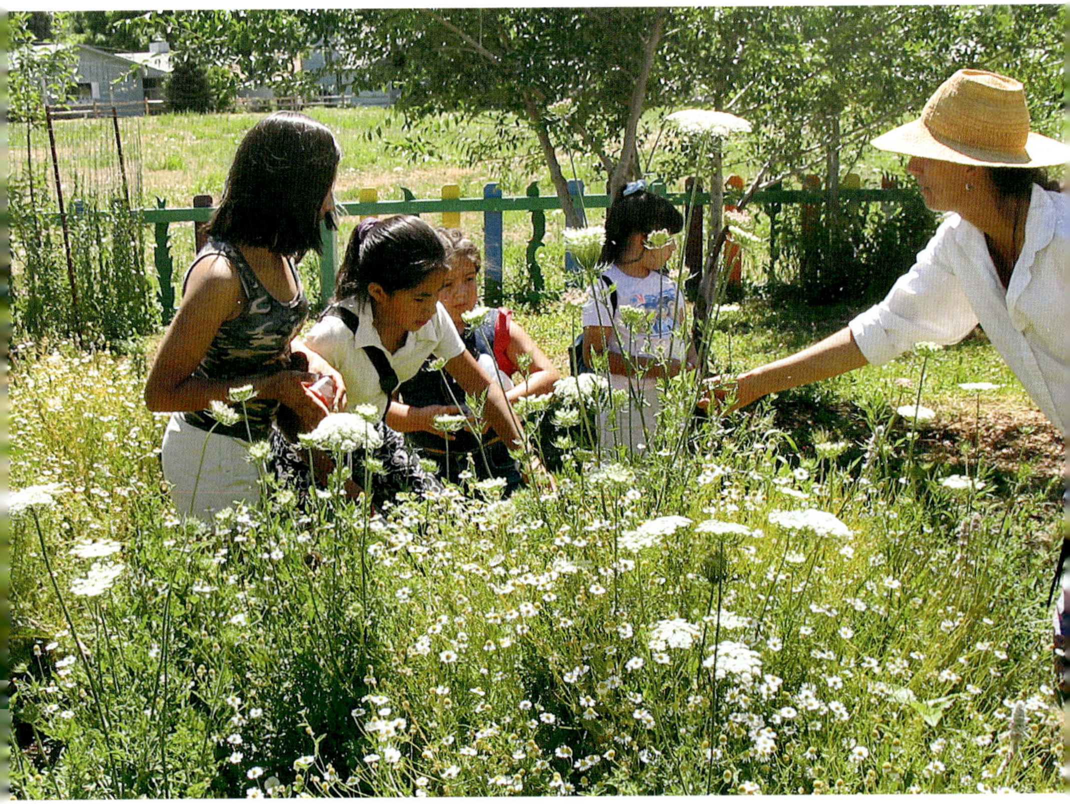

HARLOW PLATTS PARK 15

Harlow Platts Park and Viele Lake

1360 Gillaspie Drive, Boulder 80305
City of Boulder Parks and Recreation Department
303 413 7200
www.bouldercolorado.gov

Location: 1 mile from Broadway and Greenbriar Blvd.
Public Transportation: RTD Route 206 and SKIP stop on the west side of the park near the playground.
Directions: From Broadway turn west onto Greenbriar Boulevard and follow this road as it curves round Fairview High School. Turn right onto Gillaspie Drive. Viele Lake will now be in sight. Turn right into a paved parking lot opposite Heidleberg Drive at the southwest end of the park.
Parking: The large paved parking lot has about 35 vehicle spaces, and is the closest access to the playground. There is additional on road parking on Gillaspie Drive and further north in front of South Boulder Recreation Center.
Season: Attractive in all seasons. This site can be hot in summer. There is little shade in the immediate playground area, although large trees provide shade in other parts of the park.
Restrooms: Fully equipped restrooms with wheelchair access are available inside South Boulder Recreation Center during opening hours. The Center is always closed from 2pm on Saturdays. There are no restrooms in the park.
Water: Drinking fountains inside South Boulder Recreation Center during open hours. No drinking fountains in the Park.
Dogs: Yes. On-leash.

Bike some easy paved loops, look for a stalking heron, pond dip or catch bugs in Viele Lake, and enjoy the large playground in spacious Harlow Platts Park. Leave the swings to explore the small woodland nearby, then play on the bars and beams of the fitness circuit around the lake.

L ocated just south of South Boulder Recreation Center, the large expanse of Viele Lake with its woodland fringes and paved loops around the lake, and large playground set against the backdrop of the Flatirons, makes Harlow Platts Park a fun and attractive place to bring kids.

The playground is located in the southwest corner of the park 50 yards from the parking lot. Facilities include 2 ramp and slide structures, child and tot swings, and a tire swing. Recent additions include 2 areas with large boulders set in a gravel base, which are fun for climbing and jumping. There is little shade around the play area although a small shelter with picnic table is located to its side. The lake-side of the play area is fenced to prevent kids running into trail users and towards the water. Approximately 50 yards to the southeast of the playground there is an informal trail that takes you under cottonwoods and next to some dense vegetation fringing Viele Lake. This provides some good exploring and nature opportunities a short distance from your playground base.

If your outing involves bikes and strollers, choose from two easy loop trails on paved surfaces. The shorter loop of 0.3 miles goes around the lake inlet via the pedestrian bridge and can be started by the

Tips: Most weekdays the Recreation Center is open during daylight hours for access to restrooms and drinking fountains. On Saturday afternoons when the Center is closed from 2pm, bring water—the nearest public restrooms are now at Martin Park or at King Soopers at Table Mesa Shopping Center.

Other options:

1. South Boulder Recreation Center Grounds and Disc Golf Course. Try out the 9 hole Disc Golf Course located at the east side of the park and adjacent to the High School. Check out the feeder ditch that divides the park north of the Recreation Center for any bugs. Spill over into Fairview School playground along a paved trail when school is not in session.

2. Tantra Park. This is one of the Boulder's best parks for winter sledding and even getting out a kid's snowboard with its good slopes and special padding on the park trees in case of crashes. It also holds snow longer than most City parks because of its aspect. Tantra Park is located behind residential streets and adjacent to Summit Middle School at 46th Street and Hanover Avenue. However the sledding area, playground, shelter and picnic tables are located a few blocks to the south and can be accessed by driving further south along 46th and parking in nearby streets.

---

playground. The longer loop circles the lake and is approximately one mile. This loop passes next to some large cottonwoods on its east side which may prove fun for exploration as well as a fishing pier and boat jetty. Throughout the lake's shoreline there are often geese and a few ducks to watch and opportunities for pond dipping and looking at insects; bring a container or net to search for things. If your child has a fishing rod this is a good place to practice using it. There are no restrictions, although it's also said there are no fish!

Other features in Harlow Platts Park include a fitness circuit, which provides 18 stations with permanent exercise equipment set along the park perimeter trail. The equipment can be fun for kids to try out, whether balancing on beams, using bars to swing on or simply running a small car along a surface. To the north side of the Recreation Center there are volleyball areas, tennis courts and soccer pitches as well as the Disc Golf Course—see other options above. Take your time and enjoy the space.

TOWN OF LYONS 16

Funky sculptures, little bridges and lots of red sandstone. How many times have you driven through Lyons and just been aching to cool down and stretch out if you only knew how or where to turn off the One Way highway system? We describe a couple of parks with creek access only a few blocks from the centrally located Visitor Center at 350 Broadway. We also describe the seasonal Lyons Sculpture Trail which seems to be gaining momentum and popularity as a fun family outing since its inception in 2005.

Town of Lyons

Colorado 80540

Lyons Chamber
of Commerce
303 823 5215
www.lyons-colorado.com

Location: 15 miles west of Boulder on Hwy36.

Meadow Park

Location: Just west of Highway 7 (5th Avenue) and Railroad Avenue in Lyons.

Seven acres of open space bounded on three sides by the North St Vrain River and sandstone cliffs make this park an all time favorite for cooling down and picnicking.

Facilities include a playground (ramp and slide structure), restrooms, drinking fountain, picnic tables, barbecue grills, and sand volley ball court which doubles as an ice rink in winter. Meadow Park is also the start point of Lyons White Water Park—a shaded 1/4-mile horseshoe-shaped stretch of the North St Vrain Creek. Kids will love the huge stone blocks that help shape the pools and eddies of the Kayak Park but which also make great places for dipping toes, sticks or even jumping in. If the river is too overwhelming for a tot, try the child-sized stone-lined irrigation ditch that traverses the park and bring a boat to sail down it as you run alongside on soft shortcut grass. Check out the popular swimming hole at the park's north end not far from the historic low slung stone shelter. Even if you don't go in the water, the adjacent mini red sandstone cliff makes a fun play setting.

If possible visit this park midweek for a quiet trip and easy free parking. At weekends, high visitor numbers have led to a $5 parking charge, and a barrier in place means a longer walk to the river and playground. Alternatively, park at the Visitor Center one block east of the park entrance on 5th Street and bike or walk to the park. If you really enjoy the Meadow Park location, consider camping. For $15 per night, there are walk-in (50-100 yards distance) tent-only sites next to the river. Call 303 823 6150 May 1st through September 15th.

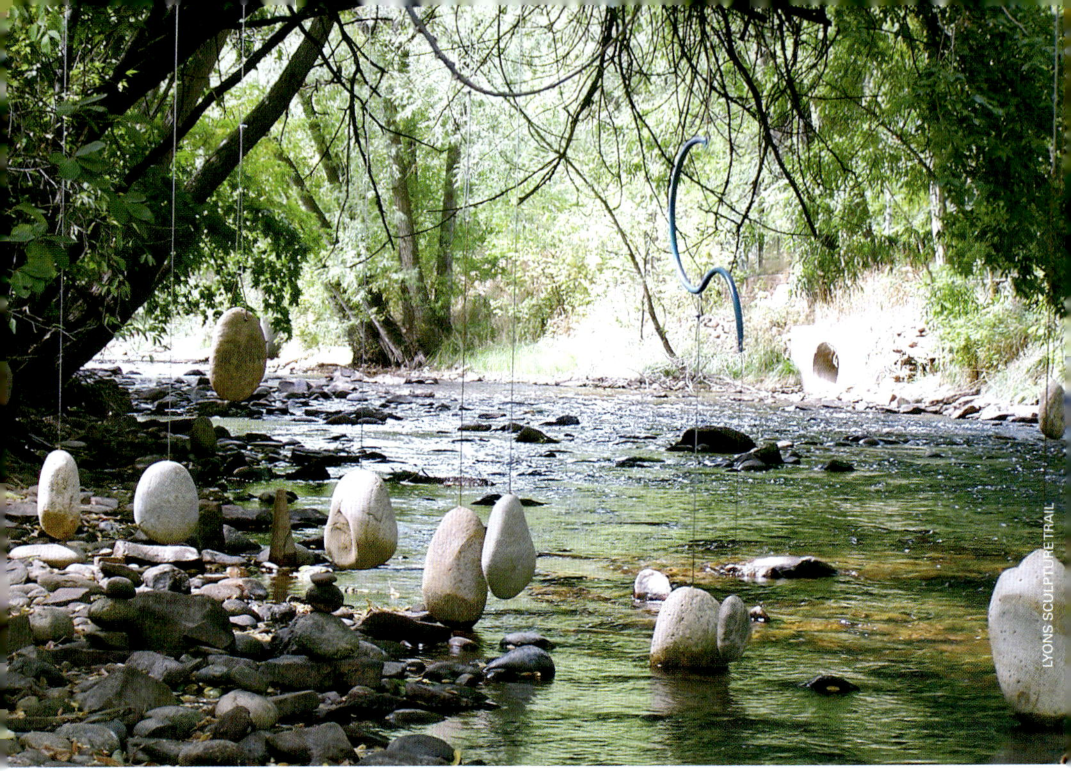

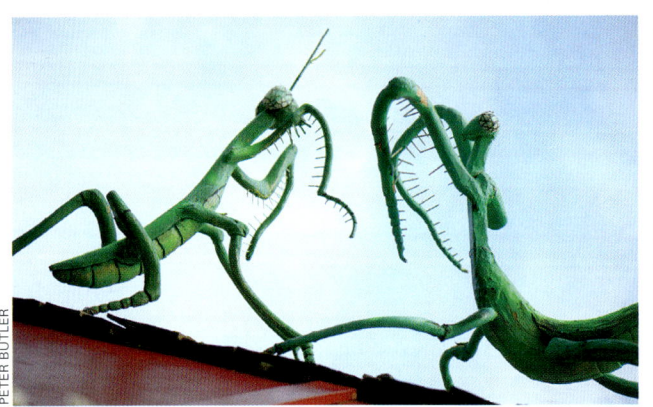

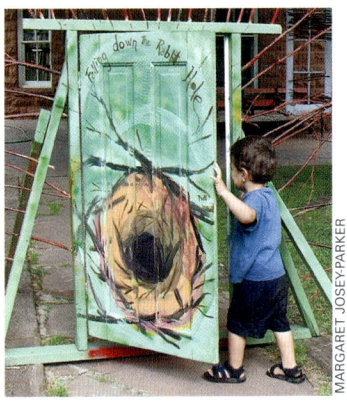

LYONS SCULPTURE TRAIL

PETER BUTLER

MARGARET JOSEY-PARKER

Lyons Sculpture Trail

Open from the third week in May until the third week in October.

Billed as "fun, inventive, interactive, and ...... nothing like art in stuffy museums", the Lyons sculpture trail is a themed trail involving more than 60 pieces of sculptural art installed amongst the buildings of downtown Lyons as well as along its parks and riverside. Since the event was started in 2005 the Sculpture Trail has gained in both size and popularity. The self-guided trail starts at The Barking Dog Café (447 Main Street) or The Stone Cup Café (442 High Street). Guidebooks are for sale ($2) at both of these locations, as well as at the Visitor Center and other places around town. The self-guided trail can be done on foot in one to two hours. While some of the theme and vision of the sculpture trail may be a little over the heads of your under 5's the sculptures are striking, unusual and best of all, outdoors. Consider bringing a bike or trike for your kids—the town trails are paved and mostly level. For more information see: www.sculpturetrail.com

Bohn Park

Location: On 2nd Avenue, south of Hwy36 (Main Street).

This is the place to bring your dog and let it run off-leash in a designated unfenced area along river frontage. The 5 acres of developed parkland and 25 acres of undeveloped parkland bordering St Vrain River form Lyon's largest park. Although visually less striking than Meadow Park, this location still offers lots of places to wade or get close to the creek including pool areas with sandstone blocks to stand on. Other facilities include ball fields, fishing ponds with accessible ramps, fully equipped restrooms, drinking fountain, picnic tables and a group shelter. The playground at the west side of the park is due to be refurbished in 2006, but currently consists of 4 child swings and a small ramp and slide structure.

To reach this park, turn off Hwy36 on the south side of Lyons onto 2nd Avenue. Follow this road south, over St Vrain Creek, to the large sandstone sign marking the park location on the west side of the road. To reach the river and playground area described, park at the west end of the large parking lot past the ball fields.

Eats and Treats

Cafes and coffee shops abound along Broadway and High Street, the through traffic one-way streets of Lyons. The Lyon's Soda Fountain on 400 Main Street is the place for old fashioned ice cream treats. The business dates back to the 1920's and still has touches of the old décor with a cherry wood mirrored soda fountain. Expect large portions of malts, sodas, shakes and sundaes and sit your child up on the counter stool for their treat.

17 MARSHALL MESA TRAIL ......

Get close to Boulder's coal mining past and learn about Marshall's underground fires which still burn to this day! Give your dog a treat and let him cool off in a ditch of flowing water at the top of the Mesa. Enjoy the views across the plains and look for wildflowers in the meadows.

Marshall Mesa Trails and Historic Mining Area

Marshall Road, Boulder 80303
City of Boulder Open Space and Mountain Parks
303 441 3440
www.bouldercolorado.gov

Location: Trailhead located by the Marshall Road and Hwy93 intersection.

Public Transportation: RTD GS Express Service on Hwy93 between Golden and Boulder stops right by the trailhead.

Directions: Enter the new trailhead parking area on the south side of Marshall Road just off the southeast corner of Hwy93/Marshall Road. This is located opposite Eldorado Springs Drive leading to Eldorado Canyon State Park.

Parking: The new 2006 parking lot has about 50 vehicle spaces. Note this parking lot replaces the former roadside parking and trailhead access 0.9 miles further east down Marshall Road.

Season: All year. The irrigation ditch only flows in late spring to mid-July.

Restrooms: Vault restrooms with wheelchair access.

Water: No. Bring your own.

Dogs: Yes. Trailhead on-leash for short distance and then off-leash voice and sight control.

Note: At the time of writing, the parking and trailheads at Marshall Mesa are being moved to the Hwy93/Marshall Rd location. The trailhead information and trail description below is based on information from the City of Boulder.

Easy to find, Marshall Mesa is a large open space area of grassland and Ponderosa Pine located on the south side of Boulder. Marshall was the first coal mining district in Colorado, and the series of three trails with interpretative signs and visible traces of past mining activity reveal its story.

This location can be busy with mountain bikers, runners and dog walkers, however we've included it for those families who love letting their dogs stretch their legs, with the added prize of the cool ditch water at the end of the trail for a hot hound. In addition it's fun to play detective and look for signs of the area's mining past. In its heyday between 1859 and 1936, there were 51 mines in Marshall supplying coal by train to the Denver Metro area. Today remnants include railroad grades, old mine foundations, and gently mounded spoil heaps now grown over with grass and small trees.

From the parking lot look for the information board and map to orient yourself, and pick up a history brochure. Choose from three trails from the parking lot. The easy grade Davidson Ditch Trail goes east along the redundant same-named ditch. Another trail parallels Hwy93 going south, and a third is a spur off this trail leading to the Community Ditch. With the addition of these three new trails there will be a good range of options for loop and combination hikes.

The trails formerly accessed from the old trailhead, which are described from the old parking and

Explore the dry ditch and look for fossil ripple marks in stone.

Tips: Bring a backpack child carrier. Trails can be very muddy after heavy rain or snow; delay your visit for 24 hours if you don't want sticky 'mud plates' on your feet. Wildflowers are good from late May through early July. Note the trail changes in 2006.

Other options:

1. Eats and Treats at Eldorado Corner Market. Not just a gas station, the Corner Market at the Hwy93/170 stoplight has a good range of baked goods and expresso coffee. Get there early for coffee (7am - 11am) and don't miss the apple cake!

2. South Boulder Creek Trail. For easy access to a lowland trail (stroller accessible for a short distance) that meanders through prairie grassland next to South Boulder Creek take a 1.9 mile trail for as little or as far as you want. The parking lot is located on the west side of South Foothills Hwy, 0.5 miles north of the Hwy93/170 stoplight. A picnic table (albeit in the parking lot!) is located under a large cottonwood next to the fenced pond and cattail area (vault restroom nearby). If you have a mellow or snoozing child in a backpack, turn this hike into a four mile loop by returning via the Big Bluestem Trail (see trailhead board for information in the parking lot).

3. Community Ditch Trail Continuation. Cross over to the west side of Hwy93 to continue along the Community Ditch Trail; at 1.7 miles it merges with Doudy Draw. Although this trail follows the ditch and is fun when the water is flowing, it is linear, exposed, and (somewhat riskily) entails crossing Hwy93 with young children.

- - -

trailhead, will remain and can be linked either at a lower level from the east end of the Davidson Ditch Trail or from the west end of the Community Ditch Trail. The Marshall Mesa Trail climbs more directly than the Community Ditch Trail to gain the Mesa plateau. Initially steep, the trail then contours up the slope at a gentler gradient, becoming more interesting as you pass exposed rock and stands of pine trees.

As the ground begins to plateau look for an interpretative sign which shows a Victorian-era boy standing amid a strangely smoking landscape; here you can learn about Marshall's infamous underground coal fires. It's believed the first fires started about one hundred and thirty years ago and still burn deep underground on nearby private land. A quiet option at this point is to leave the traffic of Marshall Mesa Trail and take the worn dirt trail to the right (northwards). This goes for a short distance onto an arm of the Mesa and provides a good place for views, picnicking or playing around the stands of pine trees.

If you remain on the Marshall Mesa Trail you reach the clear flowing water of the Community Ditch after 0.9 miles. (Note the flow is seasonal—usually April through mid summer). Pause a while to the delight of your water-loving dog. The ditch sides are steep and it is not a wading option for young children unless you find the cattlecrossing to the west. Look for the exposed sandstone bedrock under the water and watch how fast a stick or leaf races along.

For the return loop, walk west along the Community Ditch Trail until it links with the new trail next to Hwy93 and follow it northwards back to the parking lot.

18 MARTIN PARK

Peek at the creek and climb around huge dead wood branches. Visible from Broadway and yet tucked away next to Bear Creek, Martin Park provides a pleasant playground and park area combined with opportunities for getting a little wilder by exploring woodland and getting down to the creek in Bear Creek Greenway

Martin Park

36th and Eastman, Boulder 80303
City of Boulder Parks and Recreation
303 413 7200
www.bouldercolorado.gov

Location: 0.3 miles from Broadway and Table Mesa Drive.

Public Transportation: RTD/SKIP bus services stop on Broadway 150 yards from the playground.

Directions: Drive east on Table Mesa Drive and turn left onto 39th Street. Turn left onto Dartmouth Avenue and follow this to its end.

Parking: Dartmouth Avenue dead ends next to Bear Creek and the playground. Park just out of the turning circle.

Season: All year. Tall trees next to Bear Creek and the shelter provide shade from summer heat. Good fall color on the Greenway.

Restrooms: Fully equipped restrooms with wheelchair access located in the shelter (summer only).

Water: A drinking fountain is located on the south side of the pavilion next to the tennis courts (summer only).

Dogs: Yes. On-leash.

Note: The directions given are not for the park's conventional address of 36th and Eastman, because the park is easier to find this way.

The red playground equipment of Martin Park is easily seen from the busy intersection of Broadway and Table Mesa and yet this park is surprisingly tucked away behind residential streets, bordered by Bear Creek and the adjacent Bear Creek Multiuse Trail. You might want to bike, hike or take the bus, because for a first visit it's almost easier to find the park this way than from a vehicle.

From the Dartmouth Avenue parking, cross the wooden bridge over Bear Creek to access Martin Park. The playground is 50 yards from the parking lot and has 2 ramp and slide structures, children's swings, tot swings, and boulders set in a sand base. A large group shelter and barbeque area borders the playground and provides good shade in summer. To the west of the playground short mown grass allows opportunities for ball games and other activities. Smooth paved trails next to the playground make good beginner bike or trike riding, but watch out for fast skaters and cyclists on the multiuse trail.

As you follow the trail eastwards traffic sounds diminish and tall cottonwood trees provide shade over a running stream (see Tips on seasonal flow). Look for signs of recent planting and bees and butterflies; a special 3-year conservation project between the City of Boulder's Parks Department and Greenways Program is replacing short mown bluegrass turf with native grasses, shrubs and flowers. Once these areas get established the area between Martin Park and Bear Creek Canyon will be of much greater value to birds and other wildlife.

Other options:

1. Creekside Elementary School Playgrounds. The large school grounds are available for public use outside school hours. The playground to the right of the school buildings provides the most modern and fun play structures for under 5's.

2. Table Mesa Shopping Center. Located on Table Mesa Drive and Broadway. Take a short stroller walk or cycle under Broadway for eats and treats in the smaller stores on the west side. Simple options range from Mickey C's bagel and ice cream store (child sized scoops and free sprinkles), coffee and cake at Café Sole to pizza next door. There is plenty of outdoor seating and despite the large parking lot great views towards the Flatirons and afternoon/evening sunshine.

3. Broadway Trail and Bear Creek Trail. Get to know your local multiuse paths by exploring locations by bike. Broadway Trail is the arterial north/south multi-use trail through Boulder. Expect high use levels. This trail links many parks and open spaces across town. Bear Creek Trail initially goes east under US36 before rejoining open space along the tree-lined creek northwards for 0.8 miles. For more information on Boulder's Multiuse Trails visit the City website www.bouldercolorado.gov

Tips: Expect seasonal stream flow in Bear Creek with higher volume during spring runoff. This is a good sheltered location on a high wind day. Bring water in winter.

The mid to far east part of the Martin Park open space is where you find the most natural vegetation. Large cottonwoods and fallen limbs are scattered through linear shaped woodland. Look for a small wooden bridge about 200yards down stream from the playground that gives access to Creekside Elementary School. At this point the creek has been widened with large boulders and concrete floor. It provides a good solid place for small children to rock hop or do some wading under the shade of cottonwood trees. It also gives the creek a break from trampling feet if the focus is more on getting wet than searching for bugs!

19 NCAR

Follow the weather trail along a small mesa, learn about the 'brown cloud' and scramble up a child-sized boulder with a 'cave' underneath. Contrast your visit with a trip indoors to the National Center for Atmospheric Reasearch and marvel at hands-on exhibits that show how tornados and lightening are formed. Finish with a 7min video about the Center, which has great storm and space images.

National Center for Atmospheric Research (NCAR) and Walter Orr Roberts Weather Trail

1850 Table Mesa Drive, Boulder 80305
303 497 1000
www.ucar.edu/ucar/visitor.html

Open Hours: Center: Weekdays 8am-5pm, weekends and holidays 9am-4pm. Free admission.

Location: 2.4 miles from Broadway and Table Mesa Drive.

Directions: From Broadway, drive west on Table Mesa Drive. Follow this road past residential streets (1.2 miles) until it winds uphill through open space to end at the parking lot for NCAR.

Parking: Very large paved parking lot.

Season: All year. The weather trail is shaded in summer and gets good breezes. The NCAR building provides a place to warm-up, or an air-conditioned retreat depending on the time of year. Avoid high wind days.

Restrooms: Fully equipped restrooms in the NCAR visitor center with wheelchair access. No restrooms outside.

Water: Drinking fountains located inside the NCAR building. No water outside.

Dogs: Yes. On-leash, but not inside the building.

The futuristic building of the National Center for Atmospheric Research (NCAR) is dramatically set beneath the Flatirons. This location provides options for outdoor play and exploring along the Walter Orr Roberts Weather Trail, and then is nicely contrasted with a hands-on exploratory science experience inside the NCAR building that will work with all ages.

The Walter Orr Roberts Weather Trail starts on the west side of NCAR. A stroller accessible 0.2-mile trail (one way) leads you through a natural area of Ponderosa Pine to the end of the small mesa. There are great views to either side and the trail has good shade. As you walk along this compact little trail be sure to check out at least a few of the signs about weather and climate; for example the 'brown cloud' may be visible over the Denver plains (pollutant gases from cars and industry are trapped in a layer of dust-colored brown cooler air).

At the far west end of the trail, look for a large boulder about 5 feet high that appears to be split in two. This has lots of fun climbing and exploring options; scramble up the cleft to the top, or find your way round the back of the boulder to the undercut area where there is a hidden 'mini cave'. Help those unsteady on their feet.

Inside NCAR, entrance to the two floors of interactive science exhibits is free, with the Center pro-

Tips: Bring some pennies to roll into the gravity well; they spiral around seemingly taking longer than they should until they reach the center hole (if you really want to know what it's about—it shows the orbital pattern of free bodies in space moving in an elliptical pattern under gravitational forces!). Pack snow boots in winter for parking lot snow mounds or windblown drifts. In summer, skip around or play hide and seek in the airy courtyards found on three levels.

viding one of the best resources for learning about climate and weather in the Front Range. Even the toddlers in your group will be excited by the swirling cloud of the tornado that you can put your hand through, or how you generate your own blue lines when you place your hand on the lightning tube. Older children can move and manipulate exhibits showing fog formation or how eddies form in air. In addition, the walk-in auditorium provides great images of dramatic weather and extreme conditions in the 7min program 'Connections'. NCAR is rarely busy, there's easy access with ample parking, and there's always something to do. Visit this place regularly and in different seasons.

Other options:

1. The NCAR Parking Lot. Young bike riders will find many options for riding along the smooth easy grade paved sidewalks and the large courtyard area in front of NCAR entrance. In winter the snow piles from clearing the parking lot linger for many days and are great for jumping.

2. NCAR Area Trails. There are many options for hiking a network of trails in the canyons and foothills immediately west of NCAR. Trails include the Mesa Trail, Mallory Cave, Fern Canyon and Bear Peak. These trails may be an option with an infant in a backpack, or a motivated 4-5 year old, but you tend to have to walk some distance on linear paths before you reach natural stopping and play areas. See City of Boulder Mountain Parks and Open Spaces for trail and map information: www.bouldercolorado.gov. One of the more kid-attractive hikes is Bear Canyon Trail which follows Bear Creek. Start this trail from the Mesa Trail about 0.7 miles south of the NCAR and Mesa Trails junction and follow Bear Creek west to end at the junction of the Green Bear and the Bear Peak West Ridge Trails (1.7 miles one way). More simply, an outing down the hill from NCAR to join Bear Creek for a short distance for stopping places and play around water would make about a two mile round trip with a steep uphill return. Alternatively, for an easy grade trail accessible to strollers, start your trip to Bear Canyon from below NCAR at the Wildwood Road entrance to the south.

3. NCAR is a Letterbox Site where you solve clues along a trail to find a box with a stamp inside. See: www.letterboxing.org

NORTH BOULDER PARK 20

North Boulder Park

9th and Dellwood Avenue, Boulder 80304
City of Boulder Parks and Recreation Department
303 413 7200
www.bouldercolorado.gov

Location: 0.3 miles from Broadway and Dellwood Avenue.

Public Transport: RTD/SKIP bus services stop on Broadway 2 blocks from the park.

Directions: Drive west on Dellwood Avenue for 0.3 miles. You will see the park on the left side of the road.

Parking: Cross 9th and follow Dellwood Avenue, past 8th Street, until you see a large paved parking lot on the left. There are vehicle spaces for over 50 cars. If this is full, or even if it is not, many people choose to park on the residential street, Dellwood Avenue.

Season: All year. This park is exposed to wind and can be hot in summer. Near the playground area there is some shade from individual trees and under the large group shelter. A cluster of large elms on the park's south boundary provide the most shade in summer.

Restrooms: Fully equipped restrooms with wheelchair access are located on the west side of the large shelter (summer only). In winter 2 port-a-potty restrooms are provided instead.

Water: A drinking fountain is located on the west side of the playground (summer only).

Dogs: Yes. On-leash.

Meet up and play at this easy to find Boulder Park. From the playground take in great views of the Flatirons and the antics of extreme Frisbee or whatever other park activity catches your eye, then take the stroller just 2 blocks and choose from a whole host of eats and treats at the popular Broadway Community Plaza.

North Boulder Park is well known and well used and could earn the title of Boulder's most social park. It is not a park on the wild side. Crowds of all ages use this area with activities from extreme Frisbee, organized ball games, a solitary figure practicing a martial art under a tree, to throngs of parents and children that surround the playground on weekends. As with many of Boulder's parks it has the classic Flatirons backdrop.

Because of its location, you are just as likely to see people walk or bike here than arrive in a car, and the park's short-cut acres of grass are criss-crossed by paths; North Boulder Park backs onto residential areas, Boulder Community Hospital and 2 blocks away—Boulder Community Plaza.

The playground is located at the north end of the park and includes 2 ramp and slide structures, 4 child swings, 4 infant swings and a few sit-on animals. Considering the park's high use, it does not have the range of play equipment you might expect, but this does not put off the number of users. To the west of the playground a large group shelter provides shade in summer with picnic tables. Overgrown juniper beds next to the shelter provide a good hide and seek location. The paved paths around the playground and ball fields provide good loop options for bike, trike and scooter riders.

Other facilities at the park include 2 ball fields, a basketball hoop, and a wheelchair fitness court on a paved surface. In winter, and when there is snow on the ground, Boulder Nordic Club maintains a ski track around the perimeter of the park.

Tips: Bring a stroller to walk to the stores on North Broadway, bikes and trikes, a kite and water to the park in winter. Trails around the Mount Sanitas area are good for spring/summer wildflowers, even quite close to the parking lot. Bring a wildflower ID guide, child backpack carrier, food and water.

Other options:

1. Eats and Treats at Broadway Community Plaza. To get to the Plaza, walk to the south end of the park where it intersects with Alpine (streets run alphabetically in this neighborhood), head 0.2 miles down Alpine (east) to reach Broadway. Broadway Community Plaza now stretches in front of you on the opposite side of the road. Choose from Breadworks Bakery for the best brownies in town, the well known Vic's coffee shop, Moe's Bagel store—always a pocket friendly outing for hungry kids—organic fruit at Ideal Market, and for something different stop at Ginger and Pickles; a great independent toy store full of creative play ideas.

2. Mount Sanitas Bouldering and Trailheads. For a range of trailhead options in this North Boulder locality and a chance to get a little closer to nature start at the trailheads for Mount Sanitas and Red Rocks. Drive just under 1 mile west of Broadway on Mapleton Avenue and look for roadside parking. A trail that is always popular with babes or tots in backpacks is the steep 1.4 mile (one way) Mount Sanitas Trail. (Returning via the East Ridge and Sanitas Valley Trail makes a good 3.4 mile round trip with a snoozing or mellow child). The south part of the Mount Sanitas Trail is used by climbers for access to boulders and the sandstone ridge right next to the trail. This makes a fun stopping point with kids, but the proximity of the trail means that kids cannot spread out so easily without encountering trail traffic (see Crown Rock pg 42) for a similar, more kid-friendly, environment). In the immediate trailhead area near the Sanitas parking lot, a small stream provides interest and there are also options to link short paths and look for bugs and wildflowers with your reluctant walking three year olds. On the opposite (south) side of Mapleton Avenue two different trails access Red Rocks and Settlers Park from the north (pg 89). Note: All the trails mentioned are very popular even midweek, have a steep grade, receive a high level of dog walker traffic and have limited parking. For these reasons this area is not dealt with in the guide in greater detail but see www.bouldercolorado.gov for more information under Mount Sanitas.

21 PEARL STREET MALL

Achieve the impossible—chat in a coffee shop while your kids play in a sandbox complete with toys. Then eat and treat your way down Pearl Street Mall stopping at climbable rock and animal sculptures, watching zany street performers and listening to all sorts of street music. Cool off in the children's Pop-jet fountain, and if you still have the energy, finish in Barber Park playground with its pulleys and sand scoops. It's all fun and it's all free!

Pearl Street Mall — Pedestrian District

11th — 15th Street, Boulder 80302
City of Boulder
303-449-3774
www.downtownboulder.com

Location: Pearl Street Mall crosses Broadway east to west in historic downtown Boulder.

Public Transportation: RTD/SKIP buses stop near the Broadway and Pearl Street intersection.

Directions: The pedestrian section of Pearl Street Mall stretches 3/4 mile in an east/west direction from 11th -15th Streets. The Mall can be approached on foot from any direction, but see below for parking.

Parking: There are at least six parking areas highlighted on tourist brochures. Some areas are metered, others charge by the hour. Because we recommend a linear walk up or down Pearl Street, we suggest the following areas at either end of the pedestrian area; these are easy to get to, and there is no charge on weekends. At the west end of Pearl Street, there is free 2 hour parking on 8th, located between Walnut and Pearl. At the east end of Pearl Street on 15th, there is a parking garage, located between Pearl Street and Canyon Boulevard, which is free on weekends.

Season: All year. Pick a sunny day. Weekends can be busy but that's part of the atmosphere.

Restrooms. Fully equipped restrooms with wheelchair access are located at 13th and Pearl.

Water: Drinking fountains are located at intervals down Pearl Street Mall.

Dogs: No dogs are allowed on the Mall. This code is enforced.

Justly ranked as one of the U.S.'s top outdoor malls, Pearl Street Mall provides a pocket-friendly and fun outing for all the family spread out over approximately 3/4 mile. Located in Boulder's historic downtown area, Pearl Street Mall started out as a dirt street 150 years ago. In 1977 it was converted into one of the US's first pedestrian malls and since then has gone from strength to strength.

From the 8th and Pearl Street parking lot, walk east past the colorful **University Bicycles**. Test drive the bikes for tykes and check out the ornate rickshaw usually parked outside. After you have crossed over 9th, look for the **Trident** coffee shop and bookstore located on the south side of the road at 938 Pearl Street. This is one of Boulder's hidden gems for parents. Buy your beverage, and then retire to the shady courtyard at the back. Next to the water fountain sits a large sandbox brimming with trucks and plastic digging tools. Let the kids dig in while you relax. Visit on a hot day and escape the heat.

After crossing 11th, you enter the pedestrian section of the Mall. Immediately look for the giant **pillar of sandstone** with riffles of water flowing down it. Kids are drawn like magnets and allowed to touch!

Cross over Broadway (12th) and sample from over 100 **ice cream** combinations at Ben and Jerry's, or head next door for great **cookies** at the Paradise Bakery. You're now at the large **polished boulders** set in a special pit, with a mini bridge to crawl under or over. Despite their polish (or perhaps because of it) children love to crawl and slide all over these boulders. Cross over 13th and you enter **street performer territory**. Entertainment varies from the Bendy Man, who contorts into a tiny box, to fire-eating jugglers and card-retrieving parrots—take your pick!

By now you are probably hot and tired, but run as fast as you can to keep up with your kids who have just spotted the **Pop-jet Fountains**. This facility is pure genius. 28 waterspouts pop-up seemingly at random from a mechanism embedded in the pavement. Cooling and great fun. See 'Tips'. There are plenty of benches around the fountains, or you can lounge on the adjacent grass of Boulder Courthouse. After this crescendo of excitement cross over 14th and look for **large animal sculptures** of a frog, beaver, snail and rabbit in stone and metal. They are located next to a feature that presents an inlay of Rivers in the Rockies, surrounded by short blocks that are always popular as jumping posts. You are now opposite **'Into the Wind'**, a store that stocks toys and all things that fly from the fascinating to the fabulous. The extensive pocket money racks are just about affordable and full of novelty items to the delight of all ages.

Now that your tour is over, you simply have to retrace your steps (but see Barber Park Playground under other options). Bring a stroller for a swift exit!

Tips: Kids are required to wear shorts or a swimsuit at the Pearl Street Pop-jet fountain. Bring a swim diaper for the under 3's. Don't forget a towel. The Pop-jet fountains are open 10am-7pm June-September, and sometimes do not run in poor weather. Note: bicycles can only be pushed, not ridden on the Mall—this code is enforced.

Other options:

1. Pearl Street Mall Events and Festivals. Every day is a street performer and music day on Pearl Street Mall, but see www.downtownboulder.com or call 303 449 3774 for the events schedule or for more information. Highlights include the Tulip Festival in April, Pearl Street Art Fair in July, Fall Festival in September as well as parades at Halloween and for the Christmas Lights.

2. Barber Park Playground. Located on 15th between Pearl and Spruce. If your party still has the energy, or you simply need to escape the crowds of Pearl Street Mall, try Barber Park Playground. The park is located 40 yards from the east end of the Mall. Features include a tire swing, a large ramp and slide structure, 2 child swings, and the highlight—a sand station with pulleys. Use the pulleys to haul scoops of sand onto a platform, and then pour it down different tubes. The playground is fenced, has some shade on the north side, and is a good place to wind down.

SCOTT CARPENTER PARK

22

'Blast off!' at Boulder's space ship playground, which comes with a 4-storey rocket and meteorite crater to jump into. Spread out onto the grass areas, roll down the hill, and dip your toes in Boulder Creek. Finish off by being wowed by tricks and flips at the adjacent Skate and Bike Park.

Scott Carpenter Park

30th and Arapahoe, Boulder 80303
City of Boulder Parks and Recreation Department
303 413 7200
www.bouldercolorado.gov

Location: 1.4 miles east from Broadway and Arapahoe Avenue.

Public Transportation: RTD bus stop (Pound and Stampede) close to the parking lot.

Directions: From Broadway, drive east on Arapahoe Avenue. Turn right at the stoplight onto 30th Street. Take your first right into the large parking lot next to the Skate and Bike Park.

Parking: Large paved parking lot with space for over 100 vehicles.

Season: All year. The playground has little shade, but on its west side and along Boulder Creek, large cottonwoods provide relief from midday heat.

Restrooms: Large port-a-potty restroom with wheelchair access next to the playground at the south side of the parking lot. 2 port-a-potty restrooms are located in front of the swimming pool building in winter.

Water: Drinking fountain on the northeast corner of the Scott Carpenter Swimming Pool building. There is also a fountain next to the skate park entrance on the front of the small shed (summer only).

Dogs: Yes. On-leash.

A trip to a space-themed playground at Scott Carpenter Park never ceases to excite, (and it's also quite exciting for adults when they have to squirm their way up the 4-storey rocket through child-sized gaps!). In addition to the playground, there is a large grassed area with a mounded hill, which is good for catching summer breezes, flying kites and sledding in winter. Paved paths circle the playground; they are mostly flat and therefore good for just-starting bike riders, trikes and scooter riders. The south side of the park is bordered by Boulder Creek, and the paved paths link in with the multi-use Boulder Creek Trail. This side of the park has plenty of shade and good places to dip toes in Boulder Creek.

Scott Carpenter Park was named after Boulder-born Scott Carpenter, who on May 24th 1962 piloted the second manned spacecraft, Aurora 7, three times round the earth. The spaceship was named after the street corner in Boulder where Scott grew up. Enter the playground from the southwest end of the parking lot through 7 foot tall metal sculpted saucers that distort sounds depending on where you stand—always fascinating. In addition to the rocket ship, the playground also has a large ramp and slide structure, separate tube crawling structure for tots, 8 child swings, 4 infant swings, a small sit-on shuttle, a small climbing boulder and a meteorite crater with sand base for digging.

Tips: Pick up on the space theme and bring a toy of choice to play with. The hill in Scott Carpenter Park is good for winter sledding. If you don't have a sled, a thick plastic trash sack will still provide plenty of fun.

Other options:

1. Boulder Creek Trail. Bike to or from Scott Carpenter Park on the Boulder Creek Trail (multi-use) and avoid vehicle-parking hassles. Goose Creek Greenway (pg 62), can be reached 2.5 miles eastwards at 75th. Westwards, the trail reaches Broadway at 1.5 miles just after the City Park and the Boulder Farmer's Market location. Continue further along the 3.2 mile Boulder Canyon Trail to the Kid's Fishing Ponds, Sculpture Park, and Eben G. Fine Park (pg 52). Going east from Scott Carpenter Park usually means less traffic, especially at weekends.

2. Letterboxing. Scott Carpenter Park is a letterbox site; a set of clues leads you to a hidden letterbox containing a unique stamp, which can be printed in your notebook. For more information see www.letterboxing.org

3. Scott Carpenter Outdoor Pool. Swim at the Scott Carpenter pool, which is temptingly located right next to the playground. This pool is large and comes with a spiral slide but no tot-friendly shallow area. The pool is open from Memorial Day to Labor Day. City of Boulder Parks and Recreation 303 441 3427 www.bouldercolorado.gov

An added attraction to Scott Carpenter, and a good end to your outing, is the chance to take in the sights and thrills at the Skateboard and BMX Bike Park located at the north end of the parking lot. Under 5's can safely look through the railings. The skate park features a "street-course" with rails, curbs, and bowls. It's nearly always a good show and you might even see someone pull a back flip on a BMX bike. Be sure to explain to your kids as they marvel at this feat, that these days you learn these tricks at bike camp over the equivalent of foam packed half tubes and not in the back yard on a downed tree and an old air mattress!

SETTLERS PARK 23

Settlers Park/ Red Rocks

200 Pearl Street, Boulder 80302
City of Boulder Open Space and Mountain Parks
303 441 3140
www.bouldercolorado.gov

Location: 0.9 miles from Broadway and Canyon Boulevard.

Public Transportation: There is an RTD bus stop close to the parking lot.

Directions: Drive west on Canyon Boulevard for 0.9 miles. Just before the road narrows for Boulder Canyon turn right onto Pearl Street. Take an immediate left into the parking lot.

Parking: Paved parking lot with 25 vehicle spaces.

Season: All Year. The Red Rock Trail is surprisingly shaded in summer from Ponderosa Pine trees. In winter the trail gets warmth from early morning sun, which also makes the rock on the east side of the fins glow an even richer red.

Restrooms: No. Go to Eben G. Fine Park 0.1 miles away (pg 52)

Water: No. Bring your own. Nearest drinking fountain at Eben G. Fine Park, summer only.

Dogs: Yes. On-leash, or must comply with City of Boulder voice and sight control standards.

Who can resist the rocks at Settlers Park when they stick up like giant red potato chips? Scramble up a trail that goes right beside the rocks, find the huge tree with a hidden 'grotto' under its canopy, splash in the irrigation ditch and explore the strange formations at the top of the ridge with a backdrop of great views over Boulder and the eastern plains. This is a great family outing!

Striking sandstone rock formations and stories of gold bring you close to the history of the west at Settlers Park. Gold fever arrived in Boulder on October 17th 1858 when Thomas A. Aikins and 24 other miners pitched tents under the sheltering red rocks. This was thought to be the first white settlement in Boulder. Over the next year more than $100,000 in gold was extracted from Boulder Canyon. As prospectors moved on to new areas, Boulder became firmly established as a mining supply town.

Settlers Park will suit all ages. The fun part is the rocks, which can be reached within 100 yards of the parking lot. Even if your group only makes it a few hundred yards up the trail, or just explores the short Quarry Trail at the start, it still makes a worthwhile trip. The Red Rocks Trail is approximately a 1 mile round trip from the trailhead, and is good for your independent hikers or young children in backpacks. It is not stroller accessible.

From the parking lot, cross the paved multi-use trail, directly towards the striking fins of rock. At the information board orient yourself with trails. At 50 yards the Red Rocks Trail splits off to the right and a winding trail climbs to the east side of the fins. There is plenty of safe scrambling and some opportunities to peek over the edge. At about 0.2 miles look for a large tree immediately on the right side of the trail. It has a huge dense canopy with fallen limbs, which over the years has become a hidden den for countless young explorers.

Tips: Bring water and good shoes for children (and adults) for scrambling around rocks. The scrambling makes this an exciting adventure with kids. However, good supervision is required and sometimes a helping hand over rock surfaces to avoid slips.

Other options:

1. Eben G. Fine Park. Continue on to Eben G. (pg 52) within sight of, and 0.1 miles from the parking lot at Settlers Park. Follow the paved multi-use trail west via the creek underpass.

2. Letterboxing. Settlers Park is a letterbox site; a set of clues leads you to a hidden letterbox containing a unique stamp, which can be printed in your notebook. For more information see www.letterboxing.org

The Red Rocks Trail loop starts when you reach the saddle. Halfway up the trail and just before the saddle look for the small irrigation ditch. If you're lucky it will be full of flowing water (seasonal from April to July) and makes a great place to splash and cool off on a hot day (and that includes your dog!). Go either way at the saddle, (most people tend to go left). From here it is quarter of a mile to the top of the ridge where the hiker is rewarded with strange shaped rocks to scramble around and great views.

WALDEN PONDS 24

Get in the marsh! Trit-trot down the boardwalk to get a snails-eye view of being inside a cattail marsh and look for bugs in the water. Try some fishing, hike around a pond, picnic by open water and look for different birds against a backdrop of great views of the Rockies.

Walden Ponds Wildlife Habitat

75th Street between Jay Road and Valmont Road, Boulder 80301
Boulder County Parks and Open Space
303 678 6200
www.co.boulder.co.us/openspace/recreating/public_parks/walden.htm

Open Hours: Sunrise to sunset.

Locations: 6.8 miles from Broadway on Valmont Road.

Directions: From the 28th Street and Valmont Road intersection, drive east for 2.8 miles. Turn left onto 75th Street. Drive for 0.8 miles and look for the signed entrance on the left (west) marked Walden Road.

Parking: The main gravel parking lot is 0.4 miles down Walden Road next to the largest pond, Cottonwood Marsh. Space for about 15 vehicles.

Season: Attractive in all seasons. The boardwalk is fun at all times, but especially when the cattails are green and taller than your kids—late May to early June.

Restrooms: 2 vault restrooms are located at the Cottonwood Marsh parking lot, and also at the Picnic Pond parking near the entrance. Open year round.

Water: No. Bring your own.

Dogs: Yes. On-leash requirement west of Cottonwood Marsh parking lot.

MARGARET JOSEY-PARKER

Transformed and tranquil, Walden's 70 acres of wetland and ponds is a nature lover's paradise. Originally mined for gravel in the 1950's, the derelict area was purchased by Boulder County in the early 70's. From 1974 the area has undergone complete restoration resulting in the 5 ponds, contoured shorelines and native shrub and woodland plantings you see today.

This is a great place to expose your children's senses to the sights and sounds of nature. Over 170 different types of birds have been recorded at the Reserve, so you can guarantee there will be something to see or listen to. At the parking lot check the information board for brochures on wildlife, and pick up a check list of birds and a map of the area. Choose from fishing, exploring the 2.6 miles of multi-use trails around the ponds and marshes by bike or on foot, or simply picnicking next to open water. Facilities next to the parking lot include picnic tables, grills and a group shelter for up to 50 people. For those wanting to fish check the information board for details; the ponds are stocked regularly and no permit is required for under 16's. The trails around the ponds are mostly level on dirt or crusher fines. They are easily accessed with a stroller or kids on a bicycle, but not a trike.

Possibly most fun for the under 5's is the boardwalk at Cottonwood Marsh which takes you down to the water through lush stands of cattail. This is a real treat with its easy grade, short length and attrac-

Tips: Bring a bird book, binoculars and a bug collecting box. Look for the huge bullfrog tadpoles (golf ball size) at the boardwalk's low viewing point in late April.

Other options:

1. Sawhill Ponds. Visit Sawhill Ponds Wildlife Preserve for more ponds, trails, fishing and wildlife watching. The 18 ponds of the Sawhill wetland area actually back onto Walden Ponds. To reach them, turn west off 75th Street onto a dirt track, 0.3 miles from the Valmont Road intersection. Follow this track to a small parking area next to the fishing ponds. Facilities include an accessible fishing pier, a small shelter, picnic tables and vault restrooms. It is possible to make a short hiking link between the two wetland areas; a map on the information board shows connecting trails. For more information: 303 441 3240 www.bouldercolorado.gov

2. White Rocks Trail. Continue the wetland theme on White Rocks Trail where a winding trail though lush farmland, lake and wetland areas provides great wildlife viewing opportunities. Look for deer, water birds on the lake and the Great Blue Heron. The Trailhead is located about 0.75 miles west of 95th Street, on the north side of Valmont Road. Use the North Teller Trailhead parking lot on the opposite (south) side of Valmont Road. The trail is 1.25 miles long on easy ground and stroller accessible for the first half mile.

• •

tive design. Once you've controlled the kids desire to run up and down, find the special point on the boardwalk where you can get to eye level with the water and look for water bugs. Peer through the cattails and see if you can spot a red-winged blackbird's nest woven among the stalks. Listen for frogs. See if there are animal tracks in the soft shoreline mud. Scan the water for the 'V' of a swimming muskrat and move quietly, you may glimpse a stalking heron or a painted turtle basking on a log.

There's always something to see at Walden Ponds, but birds and other wildlife tend to be more active in early morning; the boardwalk may be empty and the light, sounds and smells are that much richer. Enjoy your visit.

WONDERLAND LAKE 25

Wonderland Lake—
Lake Loop Trail and Playground

Poplar Avenue, Boulder 80304
City of Boulder Open Space and Mountain Parks
303 441 3440
www.bouldercolorado.gov

Location: 0.5 miles west from Broadway and Poplar Avenue.

Public Transportation: RTD/SKIP buses stop close to the 4201 Broadway parking lot.

Directions: From Broadway drive west on Poplar Avenue for 0.5 miles. The sign for Wonderland Lake Park is on the right side of the road just after Quince Circle.

Parking: Park on the quiet residential street, Poplar Avenue. Alternative parking for Wonderland Lake access is also located at 4201 North Broadway between Sumac and Utica Avenue immediately off Broadway (west side). Space for about 30 cars—but see description for this parking lot.

Season: Attractive at all times of the year. This area is exposed; avoid high wind days and midday heat.

Restrooms: No. Go to Foothills Community Park for use of the new fully equipped restrooms open year-round.

Water: No. Bring your own, or go to Foothills Community Park.

Dogs: Yes. On-leash.

Wander around in Wonderland—a wildlife sanctuary on the edge of the city. Pour sand through holes at the playground's 'sand station', loop the lake on bikes, fish from the dam or take in the sounds of hundreds of birds nesting and feeding around the lake's shoreline.

Looking at water snails.

Wonderland Lake is a beautiful and popular open space area that serves as a sanctuary for hundreds of nesting birds and other water-edge wildlife. On fine weekends the circular lake walk can sometimes be an exercise in dodging the hoards of trail users with their strollers, bikes and dogs. However, if you pick a quiet time, pause at the playground and choose to explore by the dam peninsula, this location can make a fun and rewarding outing.

Approach this area from the quiet Poplar Avenue entrance. From the Wonderland Lake Park sign, follow the paved path for 150 yards to the playground. The alternative parking location at 4201 Broadway, though easier to find, is not near the playground, is right next to the main road, and takes 0.2 miles to reach the circular lake trail. It is included because buses stop nearby.

Wonderland Lake playground is a particularly quiet location set well back from any roads. It was refurbished in 2003 with a rubber base allowing wheelchair access to all play equipment. Have fun at the sand play station, where you can pour sand into sinks and let it fall through a hole. The only drawback is that most small children who want to use it will not be tall enough, so you may need to improvise. Other playground equipment includes a tire swing, 2 child swings, an infant swing, a grinning short caterpillar tunnel and a ramp and slide structure. There is a small shelter with a picnic table as well as

Tips: Follow the paved trail eastwards from the playground for a short 10min walk to the dam. Look for tiny water snails at the lake edge. Be prepared for crowds on the lake circuit on fine weekends, or visit mid week. Bring water.

Other options:

1. Link to Foothills Community Park. Link with Foothills Community Park via the unpaved multi-use trail, 0.3 miles one way. At the northwest corner of Wonderland Lake a trail branches off to the left and steeply zigzags up the hill. Stick with this on your bike, or push a short distance until you reach a level area and can cruise into Foothills Community Park. Choose from the 2 playgrounds and other facilities, including a fenced dog park (pg 59).

2. Link to Maxwell Lake and Park. Follow bike trails south from Poplar Avenue and the Wonderland Lake playground for about half a mile. Open space corridors lead you to Maxwell Lake where fishing is allowed. Maxwell Lake is located within Maxwell Park at Linden Park Drive, north of Linden Drive.

various benches. Towards the lake, a grass area can be used for ball games; the lake frontage is fenced off at this point, so there is no chance of a child dashing in.

A circular trail around Wonderland Lake is 1.3 miles (round trip) from the playground. Three quarters of the trail is on crushed gravel and, other than a steep step by the dam, provides an easy loop. The trail may suit jogging strollers better than an ordinary stroller but is manageable by both. For biking, opt for bike seat or trailer combinations. The loop could also be managed by your more able independent bike rider. At the north side of the lake, the trail briefly detours onto Utica Avenue for 50 yards. Look carefully for the re-entry trail back to the lake; it's easy to miss.

The east side of the lake provides a change of scene where the trail narrows, incorporates a small wooded shoreline and crosses the dam. This area does allow access to the shore (unlike the rest of the lake which is out-of-bounds), but read the advisory signs; children cannot wade, and although dogs can go in the water, they must be on-leash. At the wooded peninsula, look for the signs for the mini trail which follows the shore edge and is fun to explore with kids. Further south along the dam, fishing is allowed throughout its length. Try and catch a perch!

GOLDEN

Golden was founded during the gold rush of 1859 and was named for settler Tom Golden who panned gold in the valley of Clear Creek, although the area had been frequented by the Ute, Arapaho, and Cheyenne tribes previously. In the far distant past, dinosaurs roamed Golden, leaving a rare glimpse of the past in the form of fossils (see Dinosaur Ridge, Triceratops Trail and the School of Mines Trail).

Clear Creek provided water for milling, smelting, manufacturing, and generating electricity from coal from the local coal mines (parks such as New Loveland Mine and White Ash bear the names of some of the early mines). Early industries included a cigar factory, candy factory, paper mill, glass plant, brick works (see Peery Historic Preserve for original workings) three lime kilns (see Beverly Heights), and several stone quarries (see North Table Mountain).

Agriculture was a major industry, made possible by irrigation from Clear Creek (see Welch Ditch and Church Ditch) which also supplied Wheatridge and Arvada. The crops planted by David K. Wall in 1859 became the county's first commercial garden. Wheat crops accounted for three flour mills, and orchards and vineyards grew on North Table Mountain.

In 1870 the railroad arrived in Golden. The Colorado Central Railroad was headquartered here and served Idaho Springs, Georgetown, Central City, and Black Hawk. The railroad hauled supplies to the mining districts and returned with ore to be processed by local smelters (see Colorado Railroad Museum). Coors brewery was founded in 1873. In the 1890s, interurban rail lines also brought visitors from Denver (see Castle Rock) and in the 1870's the School Of Mines (see the Geology Trail) was founded, now a world-class institution. With the arrival of the motor car, Lariat Loop to Buffalo Bill Lookout, which takes in the winding road up Lookout Mountain, was a popular excursion. Many Denver socialites were wined and dined at privately owned Boettcher House (on site of Lookout Mountain Nature Center). Golden Gate Canyon State Park saw the last homestead claim in the 1950's when Golden still had a truly western frontier town feel. Golden's volcanoes, dinosaurs, and Mesas were used for the first cowboy films before the movie industry moved west to CA.

Today, Golden is still small and fairly easy to get around. More recent housing developments have led to 3 new parks/playgrounds. Jefferson County Open Space plays a huge role in open space provision and backs onto many City owned open spaces to make much larger areas. Golden has seen a major facelift both along the Main Street and the river. 25 years ago Clear Creek ran red with mining run-off and no self respecting parent would let their kids near the Creek, let alone swim. Now upriver screening/clean up operations mean good water quality, trout are returning, there is a new kayak park, and it's safe to swim and splash.

ARVADA BLUNN RESERVOIR

Take an outer bike loop around Arvada Reservoir through wildlife-rich grassland, creek and lake areas. Stop at the prairie dog colony and picnic near Tucker Lake. Bike, hike or fish at the inner sanctum of Arvada Reservoir and explore wood-fringed shorelines and bird-rich lands. Drop into West Arvada Dog Park for a dog-friendly outing. Check out the new 40-acre park next door for disc golf.

Arvada Blunn Reservoir

18915 West 64th Avenue, Arvada 80007
City of Arvada
720 898 7000
www.arvada.org/artsandrec/

Location: 5.2 miles from Golden Visitor Center.

Directions: Drive north on Washington Avenue for 1 mile. Turn right on Hwy93. Turn right on West 64th Avenue. Turn left into the entrance to Arvada Blunn Reservoir just past the Ralston Water Treatment Plant.

Parking: From April 1st through October 31st, the gravel parking lot at the entrance station has space for 40 vehicles. The lot is closed in winter, so use the nearby North Area Athletic Complex parking lot on the south side of West 64th or the small visitor parking lot at Ralston Water Treatment Plant.

Season: Attractive in all seasons. The site is exposed. Avoid midday sun and high wind days. The Arvada Blunn Reservoir Inner Property is closed to public access from November 1st through March 31st. The outer bike loop is open year round.

Restrooms: Summer only. There is a single port-a-potty at the Reservoir entrance station. 2 vault restrooms with wheelchair access are located next to the Reservoir in the large lower parking lot.

Water: No. Bring your own.

Dogs: Yes. On-leash on the outer Ralston Creek multi-use bike trail. No dogs are allowed in the Arvada Blunn Reservoir Property for protection of water quality.

Though many will have seen the blue glint of Arvada Reservoir and the looping paved trails around it from Hwy93, not everyone knows how to access this large open space area. Visit here for bike riding on multi-use bike trails, fishing at Arvada Blunn Reservoir, exploring shoreline and woodland areas and general immersion in a rich wildlife area.

Arvada Reservoir is managed by the City of Arvada. At present only the western part of the site is open to the public although this may change since a regional park is ultimately planned. Don't be too eager to pack a bathing suit; the reservoir supplies Arvada with 25% of its water and to protect water quality; swimming, wading and any other activities that require body contact with the water are forbidden.

Two options in this location are described: One for bike riding on the outer Reservoir Trail linking to Ralston Creek Trail and generally exploring this area, the other for fishing at Arvada Blunn Reservoir.

Bike riding in this area will best suit children on bike seat carriers or trailer combinations. Only the

Almazora family ready for the reservoir bike loop.

Kid's Derby Day

Other options:

1. West Arvada Dog Park. Let your dog run free at Arvada's first dog park. The park is located half a mile further east from the Reservoir entrance on West 64th Avenue. Turn left at the well-marked entrance into a large gravel parking lot. Facilities on the 20-acres of designated open space include a puppy play area, and secure perimeter fencing with a dog-accessible drinking fountain and a shelter planned for the future.

2. Bird's Nest Disc Golf Park. Have at go at disc golf in this 24-hole park spread over 40-acres of Jefferson County Open Space. The free walk-in park is located next to the Dog Park on its east side and shares the same entrance, but with a separate parking lot. The course features rolling grassland and tree-lined "holes" with established linking trails. This is a park for all ages and a fun place for the under 5's with the mounded areas, tall grass and patches of woodland.

3. Frustrated not to go swimming at Arvada Reservoir? See the entry for the swim beach at Bear Creek Lake Park near Morrison (pg 99).

---

most able independent young biker will manage this trail, and will probably require a push or need to walk the steep parts.

The outermost paved trail around Arvada Reservoir, the Reservoir Trail, merges at its east end with Ralston Creek Bike Trail with access year round. It is about 3 miles one way from the start at West 64th Avenue to where the trail leaves open space. Look for the bike trail start at a STOP sign between the Reservoir turn off and Ralston Water Treatment Plant. For the first mile the trail weaves on easy ground through the wilder parts of the park and a grove of cottonwoods as you cross Ralston Creek. The small bridge over the creek and picnic table make a good stopping place. Then climb up 6 steep cuts to reach the prize of the plateau. Pause here to look at the prairie dog colony and views over the eastern plains. Then cruise downhill for 2 miles past another stop point at Tucker Lake where you can also picnic and explore the area. The open space section of the trail soon ends by the new homes on Virgil Way. Retrace your steps if you wish to remain off road.

Alternatively make a loop around Arvada Reservoir with 1.5 miles of on-street riding in bike lanes, by taking a left at the start point on West 64th Avenue. Follow this for 1 mile past Arvada Dog Park, and then turn left onto Virgil Way. Continue 0.5 miles until you are just past Violet Avenue. Go right where a paved trail links into Ralston Creek Trail at an underpass with large cottonwoods. Join the Creek Trail as it heads west to enter the Reservoir open space area. Follow the Reservoir Trail in reverse as described above.

Tips: There is no drinking water on the entire Arvada Blunn open space site; bring your own. Choose a cooler day to visit the Reservoir shoreline so kids won't get frustrated about the regulations for no wading/swimming and instead can enjoy poking sticks and skipping stones at the water's edge.

Arvada Dog Park

Arvada Blunn Reservoir Site (The site is open April 1st to October 31st)

Another bike riding option is to enter the inner area—the Arvada Blunn Reservoir site. Follow the gravel road to the entrance station. There is no charge for biking or hiking non-fisherman. Follow the gravel access road for about 0.2 miles to reach a large parking lot that fronts onto the reservoir. Check out the new wheelchair access fishing jetty that extends 30 feet into the water—it makes a good sound to walk on, and there are usually fisherman to watch. To continue biking, pick up an inner paved trail which starts at the northeast end of the parking lot. This trail (apart from one 20 foot section with soft sand) provides easy riding for about 1 mile next to the reservoir's edge. There are lots of opportunities for exploring along stony spits or under large shade trees, especially on the north shoreline. The trail ends after 1 mile. From here, retrace your route.

Fishing at Arvada Reservoir requires a permit. Charges are $5 per car or $3 per bike and the site is open daylight hours. This can be a popular place, so avoid peak times at weekends. The Reservoir is regularly stocked with different fish species. If your ardent under 5 fisherman has yet to land a fish, then make a note of the Kid's Fishing Derby on the first Saturday in June. This free annual event is open to the under 16's, the reservoir is specially stocked with trout, and there are prizes galore, education materials and helpful rangers on hand. See www.Arvada.org for more information. Pre-registration is required one week before the event.

BEAR CREEK LAKE PARK 2

Thank goodness for the swim beach! Cool off and build sand castles at Big Soda Lake on scorching summer days. Choose a green and shaded picnic site along Bear Creek. Bring a bike and explore the park on paved bike trails. See the bull snake at the visitor center, put your hands inside touch and feel boxes to learn about local wildlife, and look for grasshoppers along the nearby native plant trail. If you want to stay longer consider camping or overnighting in a yurt at a budget price.

Bear Creek Lake Park

15600 W. Morrison Road, Morrison, CO 80465
City of Lakewood
303 697 6159
www.lakewood.org

Park Hours: Open all year. May - September 6am-10pm, April and October 7am-8pm, November-March 8am-6pm
Free entrance for those on foot or bicycle. $4 day fee for vehicles.

Location: 8.4 miles from Golden Visitor Center.

Directions: Go south on Washington for 0.6 miles. Turn right onto 19th Street. Turn left at the stoplight onto Hwy6. Drive for nearly 2 miles to the exit for C470. Turn right onto C470 and follow this to the Morrison exit and Hwy8 East sign. Turn left onto 8 East, under C470, and turn immediately right into the entrance for Bear Creek Lake Park. The entrance station is 0.1 miles further.

Parking: There are numerous parking options (paved and unpaved) at different picnic and recreation areas throughout the park. Request a park map at the entrance station, or check the nearby information board and map.

Season: Attractive in all seasons. Good fall color along Bear Creek. The swim beach at Big Soda Lake is open from Memorial Day to Labor Day from 8am-8pm.

Restrooms: Fully equipped restrooms with wheelchair access are located at the Visitor Center. Vault restrooms are located at Big Soda Lake, Bear Creek Reservoir, on Mount Carbon, and at various other picnic sites in the park.

Water: Drinking fountains are located at the Visitor Center and outside the Big Soda Lake restrooms.

Dogs: Yes. On-leash. No dogs are allowed on the swim beach at Big Soda Lake.

Making mud balls at the swim beach

Bear Creek Lake Park provides a great resource on the Denver Metro doorstep, with 3 lakes—Big Soda Lake, Little Soda Lake and Bear Creek Lake, 15 miles of dirt trails for biking and hiking and 2,600-acres of parkland stretching almost 3 miles. Expect contrast in landscape and activities and don't try to cover the whole park in one visit. Pick up a map when you enter the park. Large trees, woodland and shade are found at all the picnic areas located along Bear Creek, while more open grasslands are located on the hills away from the drainage.

For the under 5's the swimming beach and play area at Big Soda Lake in the southwest section of the

park will be one of the biggest draws. Bring sand toys including a pail to carry water for moats! The roped off beach area has sand and shallow water, adjacent short grass play areas and a playground with a large ramp and slide structure. Other facilities include restrooms, drinking fountains, shelters, picnic tables and a concession stand open at 11am daily from Memorial Day through Labor Day. Adults may not like the noise from traffic visible on C470, but this is unlikely to even turn the head of your kids.

Consider varying a full day here by bringing bikes and exploring the park either in the immediate vicinity (on level paved trails) or on steeper gradients to the far sides of the park and the viewpoint at Mt. Carbon. At the Soda Lakes Marina watch the paddleboats, canoes and kayaks being launched (these craft are also for rent!) and spot the water skiers at Little Soda Lake. For a change in pace, check out the wildlife education displays at the Visitor Center. There are lots of kid-friendly touch and feel exhibits including a standing black bear! Ask for a schedule on Ranger Programs and special events in the Park. Outside the Center a short circular trail on gravel has signs identifying native plants.

The picnic areas along Bear Creek provide opportunities to explore woodland along narrow creek-side trails. Fishing is permitted at Bear Creek Reservoir. The jetties at both boat put-in points are fun to walk along, look for small fish and tadpoles and watch boats being hauled in and out. Pelican Point lives up to its name as the occasional White Pelican hunts for fish, and the small hill to the east of the boat ramp provides a little scrambling excursion. Locals take fishing seriously here and a midweek visit may provide more space for your child and their fishing rod.

Camping is available at the Indian Paintbrush Campground in Bear Creek Lake Park from April 1st to October 31st for the modest price of $10 per night. With its location not too far from the swim beach, this might be just the place for that first time camping experience with young children. Further distractions include a nearby archery range and horse stables, where you are encouraged to pat the horses and pony trap rides are available (see www.bearcreekranchcolorado.com for information).

Tips: Visit midweek in summer to avoid weekend crowds especially around the Big Soda Lake swim beach. Take an inflatable raft or ring for extra fun. Pack swim diapers if they are needed and possibly swim shoes. On high wind days the sheltered woodlands along Bear Creek make good places to explore and play.

Visit Bear Creek Ranch Stable

Other options:

1. Bear Creek Greenbelt. Explore 340-acres of open space by bicycle; bike seat carrier and trailer combinations recommended. The 4.5 mile paved multi-use trail is an extension of the bike path within Bear Creek Lake Park. The trail exits the park on the east side of Fox Hollow Golf Course at the corner of Morrison Road and Owens Lane, and follows Bear Creek through the Greenbelt to Wadsworth Boulevard leading to the South Platte River. Travel through creek-side woodland, grassland and across small bridges before ending up in a large open space area with ponds.

2. Morrison For Eats and Treats. Take your snack to the town's landscaped section of multi-use trail on the north side of Bear Creek adjacent to Main Street.

3. Morrison Ridge. The climbers and explorers in your party may want to check out the bouldering at Morrison, which attracts climbers from across the Denver metro area. The short, but steep, approach paths are located on the north side of Bear Creek Road at the far east end of Main Street by the last café. The bouldering at Morrison Ridge is located along a westwards rising sandstone hogback. Kids will enjoy the overhangs and nooks and crannies, and you can help them make their own little climbs. The south facing wall is a real sun trap on a cold winter day. In summer visit in the morning before the sun hits the rock. Cycle to this location or find parking along Bear Creek Road. Note: Because of the difficult access, steep slopes and prickly vegetation, this site may not suit toddlers and crawlers. As with all scrambling sites, kids need robust shoes.

3 BEVERLY HEIGHTS PARK .....

Escape the crowds at this great little park. Quiet, shady, lots of space and with scenic views of the Mesas. Bring your trikes and small bikes for use on both the paved and unpaved park loops, and watch the big cyclists whiz by after descending the hairpins of Lookout Mountain Road. If you want to visit some wilder sites check out historic Welch Ditch with tall trees and shade or cycle up Kinney Run Trail past the old limekiln to Heritage Dells Playground.

Beverly Heights Park

Lookout Mountain Road, Golden, CO 80401
City of Golden
303 384 8127
www.ci.golden.co.us/

Location: 1.6 miles from Golden Visitor Center.

Directions: Drive south on Washington for 0.6 miles. Turn right onto 19th Street. Go 0.5 miles to the stoplight at Hwy6. Go straight over, continuing on 19th for 0.4 miles. 19th turns into Lookout Mountain Road. The park is on the left.

Parking. There is a gravel parking lot located just off the shoulder of the road. If this is full, park on Lookout Mountain Road adjacent to the park.

Season: All year. Exposed position means good breezes in the summer with plenty of shade. Can be cold on a windy winter day.

Restrooms: Port-a-potty restroom with no wheelchair access located at the gravel parking lot.

Water: Drinking fountain (also for dogs) located near park entrance (summer only).

Dogs: Yes. On-leash.

This is one of Golden's more scenic and less-known parks tucked away at the bottom of Lookout Mountain. You'll rarely find a crowd here. This neighborhood park was built in 1984, spans 3 acres, and is probably better known locally as 'the park next to the two stone pillars' (the Lariat Loop Towers, built 1917). The pillars historically mark the start of Denver Mountain Parks Open Space.

The playground was constructed in 1995 and includes 2 large ramp and slide structures. A ramp to the edge of the play structure allows wheelchair access and there is a sand base. If you arrive before 10am in mid-summer, you will get shade on the playground from the large trees. Other facilities include a swing bench—always popular with the very small, an adjacent shelter and several picnic tables.

Bring a bike, scooter or trike for doing circuits on the paved circular paths or 1/4-mile gravel fitness loop. The large open area at the south end of the park is good for ball games.

Enjoy the panoramic views of Golden and North and South Table Mountain, and watch the endless procession of cyclists testing their fitness as they ascend Lookout Mountain; they set their watches at the pillars and end their sprint at the turn off for Buffalo Bill Museum.

Tips: Bring a bike or trike, sand toys, and even a kite on a windy day. Enjoy a book on the swing bench.

Welch Ditch

Other options:

1. Kinney Run Trail and Heritage Dells Park and Playground. Link Beverley Heights Park to Heritage Dells playground in southwest Golden by bike following the Kinney Run Trail (1.4 miles). From the 19th Street and Hwy6 stoplight follow the Hwy6 multi-use Trail south for 0.8 miles until the trail branches to the right for Kinney Run Trail via an underpass under Hwy6. The trail then climbs steeply alongside a feeder creek, sandstone cliffs, dense creek vegetation and tall grassland as well as the historic canbrian lime kiln. Eventually this steep trail reaches Heritage Dells Park. Facilities at the playground include a large ramp and slide structure, a tire swing and a seasonal restroom and drinking fountain. If driving, follow directions to Crawford Circle and Kimball Avenue. It's a short steep stroller push from the parking lot to the playground.

2. Welch Ditch. For a short wander on the wild side access Welch Ditch via the bottom of Chimney Gulch Trail. This 1874 construction ditch, once irrigated 4,000 acres in Jefferson County. Water flow was stopped in 2003, which may cause trees to die, so enjoy this informal trail while you can! To get there drive north for 0.4 miles on Hwy6 from the 19th Street and Hwy6 stoplight. Look for a small parking area off the road shoulder on its west side under tall trees (also marked by a wind sock). Follow the dirt track for 0.2 miles across a field until you reach Welch Ditch. Climb around the concrete structure on your right and follow the 130 year old ditch northwards on a shaded and lush trail. Pause to admire the flume and historic valve and gate structures. Where the ditch begins to curve west up Clear Creek the informal trail ends. On your return you may be lucky enough to see a paraglider landing in the field in front of you (hence the reason for the wind sock!).

4 CASTLE ROCK

Castle Rock is a treasured Golden landmark, and one of the Front Range's best mini peaks to bring out the explorer in your kids. Hike to the top of Castle Rock and they'll reach a real summit with a great sense of achievement. They'll also be on top of a volcano with great views. Hiking distance—0.8 miles one way.

Castle Rock

South Table Mountain - North End 6,319 feet
19th Street and Belvedere Drive, Golden CO 80401

Location: 1.1 miles from Golden Visitor Center.

Directions: Drive east on 10th Street to the first stoplight. Turn right onto Ford Street. (Note: This stretch of Ford Street swings right to become a one-way system and turns into Jackson Street). Keep to the left side of the three traffic lanes, turning left onto 18th Street immediately after the Safeway store. Drive west on 18th Street for 0.3 miles until it ends on Belvedere Drive. The Lubahn trailhead for South Table Mountain is directly in front of you.

Parking: Park on Belvedere Drive. Be considerate of driveways on this quiet residential street.

Season: All year. Avoid midday summer heat.

Restrooms: No.

Water: No. Bring water.

Dogs: Yes. On-leash.

Caution: Rattlesnakes sometimes bask on the South Table Mountain paths mid-summer. Be alert. Make plenty of noise if you see one; usually these creatures are more scared of us than we are of them.

Sentinel-like, Castle Rock dominates the east skyline of Golden. Although it's a much photographed and prominent local landmark it's not widely known how to access it. This description outlines the simplest way to reach Castle Rock and is recommended for kids in backpack carriers or young able hikers. At the summit there are steep drop offs on three sides, but also a large flat plateau with plenty of level areas for sitting, picnicking and enjoying the view.

Castle Rock has an unusual history; visitors first started climbing the local landmark over 100 years ago as day-trippers from Denver. For a short period from 1915 to 1927 a light railway ran to the summit with tearoom, dancehall and observatory (old photographs can be seen on the ground floor of The Golden Hotel in Downtown Golden and on an interpretative panel to the west of the hotel parking lot). After fire destroyed the dance hall, the building was abandoned and today little remains except for some concrete steps leading the last few yards to the summit. A recent Jefferson County purchase has ensured that Castle Rock and its surrounding lands remain dedicated for conservation and open space.

Start the hike at the City of Golden Trailhead sign; the Lubahn Trail weaves upwards through rabbit brush and scrub and then, somewhat improbably, right through the volcanic cap rock that forms South Table Mountain. An interpretive sign near the start explains why the Mesas stand out high above the plains and points out Basalt columns in the cap rock. Let the independent hikers lead the trail until you reach the base of the cliff band. A path cleverly leads through this short, steep (20 foot) section. Hold the hands of unsteady little ones or let the more confident scramble up like mountain goats. The trail now emerges on the plateau of South Table Mountain. Follow the path leftwards as it curves (north) towards Castle Rock and then reaches the final concrete steps (count them!) to the top.

Indian Paintbrush

Tips: Bring a picnic or treat for the summit. Look on the summit rock surface for round bosses of rock, which are signs of the basalt rock cooling from lava and proof of its volcanic past. Bring water.

Looking for signs of cooling lava

Other options:

1. Hiking. Explore the network of paths on the mesa plateau, which branch out in various directions from the base of Castle Rock's concrete steps. For a longer 4 mile round trip hike to Castle Rock using an easier trail that is accessible with a jogging stroller, start your hike via Quaker Street. 2 trailheads start to the south on Golden Hills Road. Follow the trails at a steady grade to gain the Mesa plateau. Then go northwards until you see Castle Rock.

To reach the trailheads, follow directions as described for Jackson Street. Jackson Street turns into South Golden Road. Follow this for about 2 miles, past 3 roundabouts and King Soopers until you reach the stoplight at Quaker Street. Turn left onto Quaker Street and follow this east for 0.4 miles until the paved road ends with Golden Hills Road on the left. Park in this immediate area and look for the trailhead—a worn dirt track leads through roadside boulders and then goes east onto the Mesa. For another option with parking on a gravel pullout, drive an additional 0.4 miles north down Golden Hills Road. The pullout is on the right, just before Salvia Street. The trailhead is marked with Jefferson County Open Space boundary markers.

From the summit admire views in all directions, and imagine when there was a tramcar and tearoom here 80 years ago. Listen for ravens and rock wrens and admire views towards Denver and the Plains. Directly to the north watch red switch engines shunting on the Coors property and look out for the drop!

5 CLEAR CREEK SCULPTURE LOOP

Something to distract around every corner. Adults can walk this loop in 10-15mins, but kids will be so excited by giant trout and bear sculptures, rock hopping and wading in the creek, as well as the spiral slide in the wall at Parfet Park, that you can easily make it a 1-2 hour trip. Great for a beginner's trike/bike or scooter outing and just about manageable on foot for the 3-4 age group.

Clear Creek Trail Sculpture Loop and Parfet Park

Illinois Street to Washington Avenue via south and north side of Clear Creek, Golden CO 80401
City of Golden
303 384 8127
www.ci.golden.co.us/

Location: 0.2 miles from Golden Visitor Center, or start at Golden Visitor Center where the trail passes next to the building on the south side.

Public Transportation: Route 16 stops on Washington Avenue on the west side of Parfet Park.

Directions: Drive west on 10th Street for 0.2 miles. Turn left just past Golden library onto Illinois Street which dead ends next to the river.

Parking: Park on Illinois Street next to the tennis courts or use City of Golden parking lot to the immediate east.

Season: All year. There is plenty of shade under large cottonwoods in the summer and the trail to the north side of Clear Creek is sheltered and sunny in the winter. The loop provides lots of safe access points for cooling hot toes on summer days.

Restrooms: Fully equipped restrooms with wheelchair access are available at Parfet Park, Golden Visitor Center, Golden library, or Lions Park.

Water: Drinking fountains are located outside all the restrooms.

Dogs: Yes: On-leash.

JULIE MESSA

Clear Creek Trail in downtown Golden must be one of the most popular outings in Golden, and justifiably so for its creek hugging trail, scenic views, large animal sculptures, great wading spots and close up views of kayakers using Clear Creek White Water Park. Unlike the Creek trails in Denver and Boulder, this trail is rarely crowded, so kids can navigate at their own pace.

The loop incorporates paved creek-side trails on the north and south side of Clear Creek linked by Billy Drew Bridge and Washington Avenue Bridge as well as a halfway stop at Parfet Park. Being a loop, you can start anywhere, but the Illinois Street start has the easiest parking.

Start at Illinois Street, directly next to the footbridge, Billy Drew Bridge. Cross the bridge and take an immediate left onto the south side of Clear Creek. As you walk eastwards, enjoy peeks of the historic cabins and outbuildings in Clear Creek History Park. Watch out for the bear and two cubs, count the hens in the chicken pen and then climb large boulders before reaching the junction with Washington Ave and The Golden Hotel. Cross Washington Ave and turn left onto the bridge. Stop on the bridge and look at the interpretative signs with old photos of Golden. From the end of the bridge, a winding

Dragon at Parfet Park

paved trail draws you down to the river, where you find giant trout sculptures and the spiral slide in the wall. This is the halfway point of the trip. From here there are plenty of opportunities to spread out along the river or go up the steps into the short turf, picnic tables and shaded areas of Parfet Park. At the north end of the park there is a wonderful dragon sculpture behind an amphitheater of large boulders. The dragon is just the right size to climb over its tail or around his neck. The boulders make a fun, mini climbing area.

To return, head west using the Washington Ave bridge underpass (good echoes!), past giant butterflies and deer at an amphitheater with low walls and river access. Continue past Golden Pioneer Museum (where a trailside cafe sells ice cream!) and Golden library back to your starting point just below Billy Drew Bridge.

Note: Golden Farmers Market runs every Saturday morning from the first weekend in June until the first weekend in October offering fresh and homemade produce. Located at the City parking lot (just below Billy Drew Bridge and west of Golden Public Library). Don't miss the free horse drawn carriage rides that take you on an approximately 15min tour of historic Golden. There are usually 2 carriages operating from 9am-1pm each Saturday. Enjoy the ride, marvel at the huge working horses, and don't forget to tip!

Tips: Bring a small boat on piece of string to launch and then haul in at the giant trout next to Washington Bridge. The Washington Bridge underpass can become covered in ice creep from the river during a long cold spell.

Golden Arts Festival - Kids Area

Trout at Washington Bridge

Other options:

1. Fitness Court near Billy Drew Bridge. 50 yards beyond Billy Drew Bridge on the north side of Clear Creek, you come to a Fitness Court; balance on a bar, race a Hot Wheels car over the sit-up benches, and parents—try a few chin-ups! If you continue on Clear Creek Trail for half a mile, you pass Clear Creek Whitewater Kayak Park and Lions Park, eventually dead-ending on a gravel trail in the creek-side woodland area known as Terry Grant Park (pg 132).

2. Eats and Treats on Washington Avenue. Walk out of Parfet Park and cross the bridge, to find ice cream treats one and a half blocks south on Washington Avenue on the east side of the street. Look for Janna's ice cream or D'Deli next door which both sell ice cream by the scoop.

3. Clear Creek History Park. Located on the south side of Clear Creek, the History Park provides tours of original cabins and homesteads formerly relocated from Golden Gate Canyon. Although there is an entrance fee, the first Saturday in May is free. Walk around the site, see the blacksmith's furnace in action and visit the chickens.

4. Story Time at the Library. As with all Jefferson County libraries, Golden library offers 15min story times at no charge to young children several times a week. For the over 2's, story time also includes a craft activity. Mother Goose sessions for the 0-2 years are at 10am on Monday and Thursday, and for toddlers (2-3 years) at 10am on Tuesday. See the website www.jefferson.lib.co.us for full details or call 303 279 4585.

5. Buffalo Bill Days—Parfet Park. Visit this 3-day festival for a taste of The West held each year on the last weekend in July. Watch the parade on Saturday and go Mutton Bustin' on Sunday. Other attractions include a petting zoo, live music, dance performances and Western themed merchandise. See www.BuffaloBillDays.com for more information.

COLORADO RAILROAD MUSEUM 6

Colorado Railroad Museum

17155 West 44th Avenue, Golden, CO 80403
303 279 4591
www.ccrm.org

Open Hours: 9am-5pm (summer until 6pm).

Entrance Fee: ($7 adults, $4 2-16 years), but look for SCFD (Scientific and Cultural Facilities District) free days throughout the year and if you think you will visit more than twice a year consider getting an annual membership and you'll be able to visit again and again.

Location: 1.9 miles from Golden Visitor Center.

Public transportation: Route 17 stops outside the museum.

Directions: Drive east on 10th Street (which turns into West 44th Avenue). Continue for 1.8 miles until the Train Museum can be seen on the left.

Parking: Large museum parking lot.

Season: All year. Good shade in summer. Pick a calm day in winter and if you get cold, warm up inside.

Restrooms: Fully equipped restrooms inside the visitor entrance building and also in the separate library building. The latter provide wheelchair access.

Water: Drinking fountains are located outside the restrooms described above.

Dogs: No.

Climb on board the red caboose or haul on the bell cord from an engine cab. For all the little and big railroad buffs out there, this site has to be included because it's so much fun to explore engines, coaches and cabooses in the Railroad's park-like setting. The busy steam weekends are one of the best value loop train rides in Front Range Colorado.

The Colorado Railroad Museum has become a local family favorite especially with the great value provided by an annual membership. With over 100 locomotives and railcars, 6 steam weekends a year when you can take a ride on a live steam train, model railway layouts indoors and out, and spacious park-like and semi-wild grounds we think this welcoming place is good value for the money. It is one of the few sites in this guide where there is an admission fee, but visit on an (SCFD) free day and there is no charge.

Highlights for the under 5's include being able to clamber onto designated locomotives and play trains from the cab. There are lots of knobs to turn and some cabs have working bells with pull-cords attached. Always popular are the small track maintenance cars (also known as speeders or putt putt cars). These are just the right size for kids to climb on and operate some levers. No trip is complete without exploring at least one of the cabooses. Most are open and come complete with bunk beds, old stoves and basins.

The museum grounds are large and provide plenty of material for repeat visits. Tucked away in the southwest corner are the signals and cabooses, while to the east are the workshops, working round table and engines. Always watch for deer, or a rabbit running between the carriages. The main picnic

Tips: Pack a non-messy snack and head to the upper caboose seats for a special treat in an extraordinary location and wonder what it would be like to sleep on a working caboose. Check the website for steam dates including the Easter train, Santa Claus Special, and Halloween Ghost Train as well as SCFD free visitor days. Bring some quarters for the 40 foot indoor model railway layout—you make the trains do some loops and it raises money for the museum.

Other options:

1. Bike to the Museum from Downtown Golden on Clear Creek Bike Trail. This ride has some small inclines and is recommended for bike seat carriers and trailer combinations. The 2 mile ride goes along a wildlife corridor adjacent to the Coors shunting track (!), and takes roughly 10-15mins. From the Tucker Gulch Bike Trail just before the underpass for Hwy58, take the right fork at the bike trail junction heading east. Follow this for 1.6 miles until you see a paved trail exit linking with W 44th Avenue (mailbox with the number 17935 confirms you have the right place). Turn Left on 44th Avenue and follow this for 2-3mins (0.5 miles) until you see the train museum on your left.

area has lots of tables shaded by large cottonwood trees and a grass area where you can kick a ball. All trails are gravel and accessible to strollers, though sometimes a little bumpy.

Indoors the museum is constantly upgrading exhibits with great old photographs, model trains and historic documentation of life in the steam era. However the biggest kid attractions are the working model layout on the ground floor with its miniature towns and mines, and the Thomas play table in the merchandise entrance area.

The best time to visit is midweek when it's fairly quiet, otherwise visit either early or later in the day at weekends. The outdoor model railway layout usually operates on Saturdays during the summer. Steam weekends are always busy when a working locomotive runs loops on the half-mile track; be prepared for crowds.

SCHOOL OF MINES GEOLOGY TRAIL 7

Colorado School of Mines Geology Trail and Geology Museum

13th and Maple St., Golden, CO 80401
303 273 3823
www.mines.edu/academic/geology/museum

Location: 0.6 miles from Golden Visitor Center.

Directions: Drive south on Washington Ave for 1 block. Turn right onto 11th Street. Go to the end and turn left onto Maple Street. After 2 blocks you will see the Geology Museum on your right on the corner of 13th and Maple Street. Just beyond this building turn right onto West Campus Road; a large 1919 blue artillery gun and a sign for the Geology Trail on the corner mark the turning. Go up this road for 100 yards and turn right into a gravel parking lot clearly signed 'For student/visitor parking'.

Parking: The visitor parking lot on West Campus Road provides closest access to the Geology Trail. If this is full, or you wish to visit the Geology Museum retrace your route to 13th and Maple. There are 10 designated visitor spaces in the large parking lot behind the museum building. Although signs currently read 'permit only' and 'reserved' this will be changed. If you are in any doubt, check with staff at the museum entrance desk.

Season: All year. Most of the Geology Trail is exposed and has no shade or shelter. On hot days visit in the mornings and evenings and enjoy cooling breezes at the overlook (site #5 on the self-guided trail). In winter choose a calm, sunny day.

Restrooms: Fully equipped restrooms with wheelchair access in the Geology Museum available during open hours. No restrooms on the Geology Trail.

Water: Drinking fountains available in the Geology Museum. No water on the Geology Trail.

Dogs: Yes. On-leash.

Take a self-guided trail to look for fossils including dinosaur prints, and end up at a rock park with all sorts of textures, colors and even bore holes that you can climb into. This trail provides a good little outing off the beaten track. Visit the Geology Museum to marvel at the crystals, touch dinosaur bones and walk through a mine with drilling and dripping water sounds

The peaceful and elegant School of Mines campus sits above downtown Golden on the south side of Clear Creek. The Campus is full of surprises from its architecture, landscaped grounds and unusual sculptures, to the Seismic and Geology Museums.

The Mines Geology Trail has been used to educate geology students in the Golden area for the last 100 years. Although its focus may be academic, it also provides a great resource to enjoy with children in an off-the-beaten-track location. The trail is clearly signed and brochures on site provide detailed information. The path to the geology sites is not completely paved and goes over a rough parking lot. However strollers can mange the trail with some bumps. Altogether there are 6 outdoors sites marked on the trail guide that cover the equivalent distance of no more than 2 blocks from the parking lot. The highpoints for under 5's are site #2 which is secluded, has lots of fossils in the hogback rock formation and is in a fenced off grassland area well away from the road. Sites 3, 4, and 5 are across a big park-

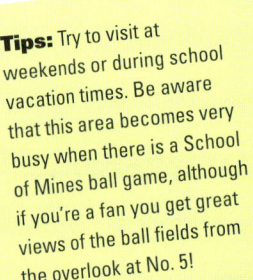

Tips: Try to visit at weekends or during school vacation times. Be aware that this area becomes very busy when there is a School of Mines ball game, although if you're a fan you get great views of the ball fields from the overlook at No. 5!

Other options:

1. Colorado School of Mines Geology Museum. Admission is free. Open hours: Monday - Saturday: 9am-4pm. Sunday: 1pm-4pm. Closed all CSM Holidays and Sundays during summer. Two air-conditioned floors display hundreds of minerals, gemstones, fossils, crystals, and old mining photographs. Most of this world-class display is behind glass, but on the lower floor there is a special walk-through exhibit, which is great fun for young people. Walk through a mine, listen for drilling and dripping water sounds and see the equipment used in the old days. You can also touch fossils, test a Geiger counter and settle down to read in a special kids area choosing from a good selection of children's geology books.

2. School of Mines Campus. Explore the plaza and enjoy shade trees, picnic areas and strange sculptures—there is an especially good one at the east end of the open grass plaza that has drill holes—where kids can play hide and seek. The plaza is located on the east side of Illinois Street between 14th and 15th streets and is one block east of Maple Street.

ing lot, but the Rock Types display and overlook to the north at site #5 make the end point worthwhile. At #5, the display rocks are large, different colors, and some are covered in 2 inch drill holes. Poke a stick through the holes or play peek-a-boo. Feel the different textures of the rocks, admire the colors and even climb inside particularly large chunks of rock with child-sized bore holes in them.

CROWN HILL PARK

8

Crown Hill Park

26th Avenue and Garrison, Wheatridge 80215
Jefferson County Open Space/Cities of Wheat Ridge and Lakewood
303 271 5925
www.co.jefferson.co.us/openspace

Open Hours: One hour before sunrise, and one hour after sunset. The Kestrel Pond Wildlife Sanctuary is closed from March 1 to June 30th to protect nesting birds.

Location: 8.2 miles from Golden Visitor Center.

Directions: Drive west on 10th Street (which turns into West 44th Avenue). Follow this for 6.3 miles. Turn right on Kipling. Turn left on 26th Avenue and follow this for 0.4 miles to reach the large second parking lot on the north side of the road opposite Garland Street.

Parking. There are two parking areas on 26th Avenue. The larger, second parking lot is paved and has space for over 100 cars. From here, the Lake Loop Trails are easily accessed by a 50 yard paved trail from the parking lot.

Season: Attractive in all seasons. Crown Hill Park is an open and exposed site. Avoid midday heat in summer, although shade can be found under lakeside trees.

Restrooms: Two fully equipped restrooms with wheelchair access are located on the west side of the parking lot. Open year round.

Water: Drinking fountain outside the restrooms (summer only).

Dogs: Yes. On-leash.

If you are an in-line skater, this is the place to tick some laps with the jogging stroller! Circle Crown Hill Lake on 1.2 miles of paved trail. Fish from shaded bank sides or venture into Kestrel Pond—a designated Urban Wildlife Sanctuary—with special viewing shelters for seeing wildlife under huge cottonwood trees.

Originally 2 small natural ponds that were enlarged into one, Crown Hill Lake and its surrounding open space span 240-acres, and hold a special place in the hearts of local residents as a peaceful wildlife oasis set within urban surroundings.

The site comprises the central Crown Hill Lake, surrounding grasslands, and the more secluded Kestrel Pond Urban Wildlife Sanctuary tucked away in the northwest corner. Circular paved and dirt trails around the lake cater to bikes, inline skaters, joggers and horse riders. Use the information board at the parking lot to orient yourself, and then pick the trail to suit your interest— most parents opt for the 1.2 mile Lake Loop Trail. This is a good outing with a stroller and rewarding for children who can manage the loop independently on bikes. There are plenty of places to get close to the water, often under the shade of trees. The lake is stocked with fish (State fishing regulations apply; no license is required for under-16 year olds to fish).

The Kestrel Pond trail at the northwest corner of the Park is an easy quarter-mile loop for young children. The marsh attracts nesting birds and wildlife. Approach the viewing shelters quietly and you may see a turtle basking on a rock or a heron fishing. Look for tracks left by squirrels, foxes and deer on the pond's shoreline.

Other facilities at Crown Hill park include a fishing jetty and a fitness circuit that both cater to wheelchair users. There are also two small shade shelters with picnic tables; one at the main parking lot on 26th and the other outside the Wildlife Sanctuary.

Tips: Bring drinking water in winter. Bring a fishing rod. For novelty, transport toddlers in a pull along wagon around the lake loop.

Play along the Fitness Circuit

Paramount Park

Other options:

1. **Events at Crown Hill Park.** Organized by Jefferson County Open Space. www.jeffco.us/jeffco/openspace_uploads/lmnc_public_program_schedule_ . In May there are several all ages drop-in 'Migration Celebration' days, which focus on sighting and learning about migratory birds.

2. **Paramount Park.** If you want to incorporate a small playground into your visit, cross over Kipling Street at the west side of the open space to reach Paramount Park. This park includes a ramp and slide structure, 2 child swings, and a shelter with picnic table. There are 2 fully equipped restrooms with water fountains located next to the playground (summer only). Vehicle parking is located on the quiet residential street Paramount Parkway. Access this road from the west side of the 26th Avenue and Kipling Street intersection. You can do this by bike, but you will need to cross the busy Kipling intersection.

DINOSAUR RIDGE 9

Dinosaur Ridge Visitor Center and Trail

16831 West Alameda Parkway, Morrison, CO 80465
Friends of Dinosaur Ridge
303 697 3466
www.dinoridge.org

Open Hours. Visitor Center: 9am-4pm Monday to Saturday, and 12pm-4pm on Sunday. Entrance is free. The Dinosaur Ridge Trail is open dawn to dusk.

Location: 6.5 miles from Golden Visitor Center, near Morrison.

Directions: Go south on Washington for 0.6 miles. Turn right onto 19th street. Turn left at the stoplight onto Hwy6. Drive south for 1.3 miles. Turn right onto Heritage Road. Follow Heritage Road and turn left onto East Hwy40. Go a short distance and turn right onto Rooney Road. Follow this over C470, and then as it takes a sharp right, all the way down the hill until it ends at the junction with West Alameda Parkway. Turn left and you will see a dinosaur sign for the Visitor Center on your left.

Parking: Paved parking lot at the visitor center for over 50 cars. On the Dinosaur Ridge Trail on West Alameda Parkway, there are a few off road parking spots, including some near the 'Dinosaur Freeway'.

Season: All year. However this location is exposed and the first half of the southeast facing Dinosaur Tour can get very hot! Avoid midday sun or a high wind day. Note: There is some good shade under screens at the Visitor Center and over the dinosaur dig.

Restrooms: Two vault restrooms with wheelchair access are located in the Visitor Center parking lot. There are no restrooms on the 1 mile Dinosaur Ridge self-guided tour.

Water: Bottled water available for purchase at the Visitor Center.
Dogs: Yes. On-leash.

Visit a 'dinosaur freeway' and see the tracks of two different dinosaurs running side by side. Can you tell which way they were going? Back at the visitor center, excavate for T-Rex bones at a special 'dig' site, and have your photo taken next to a multicolored herd of Stegosaurus. Whatever your level of interest, this world famous site can be taken as simply or as seriously as you like.

Dinosaur Ridge is one of the world's most famous dinosaur locations. Stretching for 3.5 miles between I70 and the town of Morrison to the south, the hogback spine of sedimentary rock has borne important fossil discoveries. In 1877 the first finds of Brontosaurus and Stegosaurus were made sparking a historic 'dinosaur rush' across the United States.

Today, the Friends of Dinosaur Ridge, a non-profit organization, protects the natural resources and serves as an education resource. Most people visiting Dinosaur Ridge stop at the Visitor Center, gather information, and then go on a self-guided tour of the interpretative 'Dinosaur Ridge Trail', a 2 mile round trip stretching along the hogback road.

This location attracts some 70,000 people a year ranging from families with toddlers to academics. Tailor your visit to suit your child's level of interest. At the Visitor Center, kids will be drawn to the colorful stegosaurus sculptures stalking the grounds (Stegosaurus is the Colorado State Fossil!). Run

Tips: Bring 'excavating tools' for extra fun at the dinosaur 'dig'— a small pail, shovel and paintbrush for example. Look for the painted dinosaur tracks at the Visitor Center and follow them round the grounds. Bring plenty of water in summer (enabling you to avoid the lure of the dinosaur merchandise....).

around, and then check the mini interpretative signs leading to the fossilized bone on display. Have a snack under shade at picnic tables next to the visitor center and then dig in the special Tyrannosaurus Rex excavating pit. In the same area enjoy watching birds visiting the permanent feeders: you'll get great views of chickadees and rosy sparrows.

A new Education Center is due to be opened in 2008 in the Center's renovated barn. For the time being, samples of fossilized bones and rocks are on display in the Visitor Center. However, be aware that the exhibits are dwarfed by the bulging shelves of dinosaur-themed merchandise. Much of this is great fun with the sales supporting a good cause, so you may, or may not, wish to give in to your insistent toddler.

For the Dinosaur Ridge Trail, orient yourself at the information board and pick up a brochure. Make sure you bring a stroller as the 2 mile round trip could be too long for the under 5's. However, treating

Students at the Dinosaur Freeway

the 'Dinosaur Freeway' as an end point is half the distance, and you still get to see the impressive 145 million year old dinosaur tracks, as well as palm fronds and ripple marks. One drawback to this area is that the highway has narrow shoulders and sometimes, fast cars. If you want to enjoy the trip with no road traffic, visit on 'Open Ridge Days'. These are held on the first Saturday of each month from May to October when Alameda Parkway is closed to vehicles. For a small fee you can walk the entire trail but then get a bus ride back to the Visitor Center.

As an alternative to walking from the Visitor Center, you can take your vehicle to a designated off highway parking point, and then spread up or down to look at the points of interest. If you choose this option, pick a quiet day and avoid peak weekend times.

For more information on Open Ridge Days, free guided tours and special events see www.dinoridge.org

Other options:

1. Morrison Eats and Treats. Nearby Main Street Morrison is lined with restaurants and cafés, and on the south side there is a multi-use bike path with seats and shade next to Bear Creek. www.town.morrison.co.us/

2. Discovery Park Playground. Disappointed not to climb on the Stegosaurus sculptures at Dinosaur Ridge? Then take your kids to Discovery Park, 5 miles away, where they can climb over or under a 15 foot version to their heart's content (pg 155).

3. Red Rocks Park. The stunning natural amphitheatre of Red Rocks Park is just over the hogback ridge of the Dinosaur Trail. However no climbing or scrambling is allowed on the park rock outcrops whatsoever, which is exactly what most under 5's want to do. Placate them on a non-concert day by letting them run over the large stage and rows of seats. See: www.redrocksonline.com/pages/visiting/park_trails.html

4. Dakota Ridge Trail. Hike up the spine of the Dinosaur Ridge hogback away from the road. From the Dakota Ridge Trail you get great views both towards Red Rocks and the Denver plains. This is a Jefferson County Open Space trail; see www.co.jefferson.co.us/openspace for trailhead information.

FAIRMOUNT PARK 10

Fairmount Park

5222 Quaker Street, Golden, CO 80403
Prospect Recreation and Park District
303 424 2346
www.prospectdistrict.org

Location: 3.9 miles from Golden Visitor Center.

Directions: Go east on 10th Street, (which turns into West 44th Avenue). Turn left after 1.6 miles (just after CO58 overpass) onto Easley Road. Turn right at the stop sign. Follow this as it contours around the base of North Table Mountain and turn right after 2 miles onto W. 54th Avenue. Turn right onto Quaker Street. Fairmount Park is located 100 yards on the left.

Parking: Paved parking lot for 60 vehicles.

Season: All year. Reasonable shade in summer provided next to the playground from trees and shelters.

Restrooms: Large vault restrooms with wheelchair access and sink with cold water faucet (summer only). In winter a port-a-potty is located in the parking lot—no wheelchair access.

Water: Drinking fountain on wall outside the restrooms (summer only).

Dogs: Yes. On-leash.

A cheerful and ornate sign greets you at this large park on the east side of North Table Mountain. Fairmount Park provides a typical playground outing in a quiet tucked away setting. Bring bikes and trikes for short loops on paved trails. Walk or take a stroller around the additional half-mile loop trail and play in the tall grass and trees in a wilder setting.

Fairmount Park is one of the largest parks on the east side of North Table Mountain, quietly tucked away down dead end streets and surrounded by a mix of horse properties and relatively new housing. Its 19+ acres provide a mix of formal park and tall meadow grassland left uncut for wildlife.

The playground is located next to the parking lot and consists of a large ramp and slide structure and 2 child swings set in a wood chip base. A ramp leading to the play structures provides wheelchair access.

Other facilities include 3 shelters with picnic tables, grills and a horseshoe court. The shelters are available for group use, which may make this site busy when they are booked on summer weekends. Large mown grass areas accomodate ball games and kite flying. There is a well-used horse arena in the center of the park that makes for fun viewing when it is in use.

Easy paved paths around the playground provide opportunities for just starting bike and trike riders. For the more able bikers or those with strollers/jogging strollers there is a half-mile walking trail on a gravel base. This takes a winding track around the perimeter of the park and allows you to explore the wilder tall grass areas.

Tips: Wherever tall grass borders the trail, look for insects and wildflowers. Bring a clear plastic container with lid to look at anything you come across, a magnifying glass, and even a child's large picture field guide.

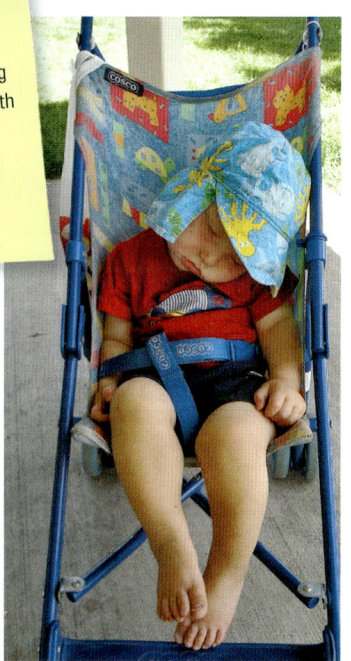

Other options:

1. Pumpkin Festival. Check out Fairmount District's annual Pumpkin Festival held at the park at 10am on the second Saturday in October. This is a popular event with lots of free and fun activities for kids including pony rides, hay wagon rides, fire trucks, give away pumpkins, and even a free pancake breakfast.

2. Fire Crusher Trail. Link to Tony Grampsas Park (pg 150), by bike or foot via Fire Crusher Trail (approximately 1 mile). Start from the southwest end of Fairmount Park (near the horse arena) at 52nd Place and Quaker Street. Go south on Quaker Street for two blocks and cross over 50th Street. Continue on Quaker Street for 50 yards to the City of Golden Trailhead sign, and the start of the off-road Fire Crusher Trail.

GOLDEN CLIFFS PRESERVE 11

Golden Cliffs Preserve

North Table Mountain
Peery Parkway
Golden CO 80403
The Access Fund/City of Golden/Jefferson County Open Space
303 384 8127
www.ci.golden.co.us/

Location: 1.3 miles from Golden Visitor Center.

Directions: Drive east on 10th Street to the first stoplight. Turn left onto Ford Street. Turn right onto 7th Place. After 0.1 mile this curves left onto Boyd Street. Follow Boyd Street up the hill and around the right bend which turns into Plateau Parkway. Take the immediate left for Peery Parkway and follow this road as it curves to the right and then straightens. At its cul-de-sac end you see the clearly signed entrance to Golden Cliffs Preserve. Take the lower of the two approach roads for 0.3 miles to the end.

Parking: Unpaved parking lot with about 40 vehicle spaces. If this is full (unlikely) use the overflow parking lot. Weekends can be busy especially during early summer and fall.

Season: Facing southwest, Golden Cliffs Preserve can be too hot in the summer months but wonderfully warm on a calm sunny day from fall to early spring. Bring plenty of water.

Restrooms: Vault restroom at the parking lot with wheelchair access.

Water: No.

Dogs: Yes. On-leash.

Note: Only experienced climbers should take children climbing; parties with no climbing experience should ask at local outdoor stores about opportunities to learn.

If you rock climb and are looking for a local site to take your kids, consider this sunny option. If you don't climb, it's still fun to wander up and see what's going on. If you still have energy take the zigzag trail through the cliff bands, arrive on the Mesa Plateau and then take in summit views from North Table Mountain. Hiking distance from trailhead to cliff base is roughly 0.45 miles, and just under 1 mile to the summit.

JOAN TERRILL

A t first glance this is not a place to bring small people, but whether or not you enjoy climbing, you'd be surprised at the number of families that make it up here simply wanting to look more closely at what goes on. The hike to the cliff base is reasonably short, though steep, and kids always enjoy the action, the ropes and all the other jangling equipment.

Climbing at Golden Cliffs takes place on basalt rock that is exposed along the southwest edge of North Table Mountain. In some places cliff sections of columnar rock reach 150 feet high, while at the far ends it tapers off to just 15 feet. There are around 200 rock climbs that range in technical difficulty from 5.6 and up. For the under 5's it will mostly be a case of putting up a top rope and creating your own 5th class mini climbs.

The Golden Cliffs Trail starts behind the information board in the parking lot. It is fairly steep so use a backpack carrier for younger children. Pause at the turns for views of the Coors Brewery, red switch trains shunting railcars in the yards and views in three directions. Watch for birdlife (over

Tips: Bring a trekking pole (or walking stick) for the steep approach trail—both you and your young independent hikers will appreciate it. Pick up on the climbing theme and let them carry a piece of rope or a sling to fire their imagination and speed them up the ascent! Child-friendly binoculars are handy for watching wildlife and climbers. Don't forget water. Guidebook: Classic Rock Climbs Golden Cliffs, Colorado, 1997, Pete Hubbel.

Summit of North Table Mountain

Other options:

1. Hike to the Summit of North Table Mountain via Mesa Top Scenic Loop Trail. Hiking distance: 0.43 miles from trail junction to summit. For those who wish to continue hiking and summit North Table Mountain (6459 feet), take a great little trail through the cliff bands to link to the Mesa Plateau, from where established trails lead to the summit. To access the Mesa Top Trail follow the cliff base trail to the right (east) until you see carefully built stone walls terraced into the hillside. Follow this tight zigzag trail through the cliff bands (if you look down your trail should be in a direct line above the parking lot). When you reach the plateau follow a trail in a northeast direction (Caution: you should be several hundred yards away from the cliff edge) until it loops around and leads you to the top of North Table Mountain.

2. Overflow Parking Lot Area. For a low-key option go directly from the Golden Cliffs entrance to the overflow parking lot. This is always a quiet location. Enjoy the views and cliff setting and turn your trip into a bug-hunting excursion in the tall grassland or explore nearby boulders. Some shade is provided by taking a short loop walk into the small wooded area to the east (this merges with the trail from the other parking lot) and then heading back.

50 different types use this area) and on a quiet day you may catch a glimpse of mule deer browsing the shrub vegetation.

After 0.45 miles you reach a trail at the base of the cliffs where you can go left or right. If you are staying for a while, pick a level area for a base set back from the main cliff base trail; there are some good places if you turn right. Be aware that the narrow paths have loose rock and sometimes prickly vegetation which may not suit your toddler. Set up a top rope, picnic and watch the climbing. Listen for rock wrens and their distinctive shrill call and look for violet-green swallows skimming for insects.

GOLDEN GATE CANYON I

12

Golden Gate Canyon State Park

Panorama Point Loop Trail and Dude's Fishing Hole

2207 Gap Road, Golden, CO 80403
Colorado State Parks
303 582 3707
www.parks.state.co.us

Open Hours: Sunrise to sunset. $5 fee for vehicles.
Location: 19 miles from Golden Visitor Center.
Directions: Go north on Washington Avenue for 1 mile. Turn right on Hwy93. Turn left at the stoplight onto Golden Gate Canyon Road and follow this for about 14.2 miles. Turn right onto Mountain Base Road. Follow this steep and twisting road to its end at the junction with Gap Road. Turn right and drive for 0.4 miles to turn left for Panorama Point.
Parking: Paved parking lot for up to 15 vehicles next to the Observation Deck. On the opposite side of Gap Road there is a dirt shoulder with space for about 10 vehicles.
Season: Elevation approximately 9,500 feet. Expect snow on the trails until at least late April. Warmer months for visiting span from May through September. Expect great fall color from the aspens from mid September. Due to elevation, temperatures can be 20 degrees lower than the plains.
Restrooms: 2 vault restrooms at the east end of Panorama Point parking lot.
Water: No at Panorama Point. Yes at Aspen Meadow Campground.
Dogs: Yes. On-leash.

Cool off on a hot plains day by hiking one of these two trails perched in the upper reaches of Golden Gate Canyon State Park. Check out the 100 mile panoramic view of the Continental Divide from a fun wooden observation deck, then take either trail for a little or as far as you want to enjoy grassland wildflowers, fall color, old cabins, mountain streams and fishing ponds.

CATHY KOWITZ
Panarama Point Outlook

F or wildflower meadows, fall color and stunning views of over 100 miles of the Continental Divide explore the upper reaches of Golden Gate Canyon State Park. Two trails are described; Panorama Point, a 2.5 mile loop trail with some steep sections, and Dude's Fishing Hole, a quarter mile out-and-back trail to a fishing pond. Both provide contrasting scenery and give you a sense of the wilder side of Golden Gate Canyon State Park.

Start your visit to the upper part of Golden Gate Canyon State Park at Panorama Point Observation Deck. The stunning panoramic views of the Colorado Rockies should not be missed. The large and shaded wooden observation deck provides a fun environment for unsteady walkers to stretch their legs, and the handy built-in benches help catch some falls. Look for display panels on wildlife observation. On fine weekends a telescope is staffed by volunteer rangers; they will help all ages look through the telescope and identify peaks on the Continental Divide.

Tips: Drink plenty of water to avoid altitude headaches. Be sure to bring hats, sunscreen and wind-proof clothing for layering; although the sun can be intense at this altitude it can be cooler than you might expect. Listen for the whirring buzz of the Broad-tailed Hummingbird and look for the flash of iridescent green on its back as it whizzes by. Bring a fishing rod for Dude's Fishing Hole.

Right: Outcrops near trailhead for Dude's Fishing Hole
Below: At the beach

Panorama Point Loop Trail via Raccoon Trail

One of the most popular family hiking loop trails, Raccoon Trail, starts from Panorama Point at the far side of the parking lot next to the restrooms. The 2.5 mile trail passes through different landscapes providing contrast and diversion for those wanting to climb out of child carriers as well as your more able hikers. Don't be put off by the first quarter mile. Fire mitigation projects (i.e. tree thinning and removal to reduce fuel and wildfire risk) along Gap Road have recently made the start of the trail a little bleak. Bear with this over the next two years as the vegetation grows back. Shortly after the tree thinning you come to a clearing with a small stream, wildflower meadow and aspen groves. In June the meadows are bright with Indian Paintbrush and penstemons. The first half of the trail then winds down the valley past boulder fields and smooth-trunked aspen until it eventually crosses a footbridge and small stream. Pause here. Watch and listen for the black, tufted ear, Abert's Squirrel. From this low point the trail then climbs back through coniferous forest. Take a left turn where it joins with an incoming trail from Reverend's Ridge Campground, and then zigzag beneath Panorama Point with increasingly good views of the Continental Divide. Most independent hikers will enjoy the first part of the trail with its easy downhill gradient, but may need coaxing, carrying or even bribing up the last steep zigzags to the trail's end. Be prepared.

Dude's Fishing Hole

Dude's Fishing Hole hike via Snowshoe Hare Trail

As an alternative to the Panorama Point circuit, this much shorter (quarter mile one way) Dude's Fishing Hole hike via Snowshoe Hare Trail provides an easier outing with your less able independent hikers. The short 10-15min hike also means you don't need to bring a child backpack carrier. Explore large granite boulders, aspen groves, an old homestead and a fishing pond with a sandy beach.

From Panorama Point drive east along Gap Road for 1.4 miles and look for the Aspen Meadows Campground turn off on the right. Drive down the campground road for about 0.2 miles, and then take a steep right turn following signs for Dude's Fishing Hole. The road loops round. Look for trailhead parking for 10 vehicles on the right side. The nearest toilets to this trailhead are at Twin Creek Loop. Water is located at the Conifer Loop section of the campground some distance away.

On arrival, and just a few hops away from the parking lot, few kids will be able to resist the large lichen-crusted boulders with their scrambling potential and small nooks. Enjoy this area, check out the view but watch the drop off.

Look for the Snowshoe Hare Trailhead by the information board at the south end of the parking lot. Follow this downhill all the way, at first through conifer forest, then along a dirt track lined by aspens until you arrive at an old homestead site with grassland meadow and the small lake of Dude's Fishing Hole beyond. The log walls of the 1890's hay barn are all that remain of Tom Belcher's three-room house, blacksmith shop and steam-powered sawmill on this site. At the lake options range from fishing, playing on the sandy beach or doing a loop walk around the lake to explore granite boulders and a mini-cliff on the north side. The pond contains lots of undersize trout and plenty of minnows.

13 GOLDEN GATE CANYON 2

Don't miss 12,000-acres of mountain country on Golden's doorstep. Feed giant Rainbow Trout at the Visitor Center, skip around the small pond loop, and go inside for lots of hands-on exhibits about the Canyon's wildlife and history. Either find the loop trail behind the Visitor Center, or follow the twisting Ralston Creek Trail a short distance to reach the quiet Ranch Ponds for fishing, pond dipping, picnicking and campfire fun.

Golden Gate Canyon State Park

Visitor Center and Ranch Ponds

92 Crawford Gulch Road, Golden, CO 80403
Colorado State Parks
303 582 3707
www.parks.state.co.us

Open Hours: Visitor Center: 9am-4pm (winter) 8am-6pm (summer). Park: Sunrise to sunset. $5 fee for vehicles.

Location: 13.9 miles from Golden Visitor Center.

Directions: Go north on Washington Avenue for 1 mile. Turn right on Hwy93. Turn left at the stoplight onto Golden Gate Canyon Road and follow this for 13.5 miles to the Visitor Center on the right.

Parking: Paved parking lot next to the Visitor Center with space for about 25 vehicles.

Season: Expect snow on the trails until at least late April. Warmer months for visiting span from May through September. Due to elevation, temperatures can be 20 degrees lower than the plains.

Restrooms: Fully equipped restrooms with wheelchair access inside the Visitor Center.

Water: Drinking fountain located inside the Visitor Center next to the restrooms. Outdoor hand-operated pumps can be found at various points located down Crawford Gulch Road towards Ranch Ponds (summer only).

Dogs: Yes. On-leash.

Ranch Ponds

The 12,000-acres of Golden Gate State Park provide a wild and scenic retreat just west of Golden with aspen groves, wildflower meadows, rock outcrops, old homesteads, and mountain streams plus the bonus of cool summer temperatures. The park is spanned by over a dozen designated trails for hiking, biking and backcountry access. The challenge as a first time visitor is finding locations and trails that make sense to the age and abilities of young children. Described are two locations from around 8,000 feet elevation that can be reached soon after entering the State Park.

The Visitor Center provides plenty of fun and activities. One of the main attractions for kids is feeding the fish. Scoops of food are dispensed from a twist machine just inside the Visitor Center doors for 25 cents. Watch the Rainbow Trout thrash, jostle, twist and leap just as they might for flies. When you tire of this, stroll the 10min self-guided loop round the pond on a smooth paved trail. The Wilbur and Nellie Larkin Trail is themed around mountain streams and wildlife and has new interpretative signs with push button and touch displays. It manages to cross 5 wooden bridges in its short length!

Inside the Visitor Center tour the many interactive exhibits. Favorites include the 'wildlife jukebox'—push a button and listen to the sound over a telephone, the sniff boxes of elk and beaver scent and the 'Who did it?' tracks and poop touch board (of course they're not real!). This is the time to pick

Below: Feed the trout
Right: Short forest loop behind Visitor Center

up trail guides and ask questions. The Center also stocks outdoor guides and some merchandise.

If you don't want to drive any further and are looking for an additional short hiking loop that gives a mountain forest experience, then take the half mile nature trail behind the visitor center. This is not described on brochures but is well-known by the staff. Start at the east end of the parking lot furthest away from the Visitor Center and look for signs for the Ralston Creek Trail. Follow this for 0.2 miles, then take a right onto Black Bear Trail, and then right again for the remainder of the trail as it doubles back behind the Visitor Center. Small plaques identify the trees and shrubs in front of you. The twisting dirt trail with its small climbs and descent will give a sense of achievement for a young hiker, and for those who can't quite make it, it's not too far to carry them to the end of the trail!

From the Visitor Center, Ralston Creek runs east paralleled by Crawford Gulch Road. Along this stretch there are many options for parking and then exploring trails although some picnic areas are close to the road and you will need to watch kids for passing traffic. **Ranch Ponds** provides an easy short hike with the bonus that this section of the Ralston Creek Trail is separated from the road by the creek. The slightly hidden and twisting trail gives a sense of exploration, with the ponds at the end contrasting nicely with the wooded start. Park at the first signed pull-in for Ranch Ponds, 2.7 miles down the road from the Visitor Center. Cross a small wooden bridge and then follow a wooded trail next to the creek (downstream) as it passes a series of small dams with lush wetland vegetation. The first pond is at 0.2 miles and the second at 0.4 miles. Try some fishing, look for dragonflies or just dabble with a stick. On your return take note of the fire pits, which can be used year round unless posted. If you want to make a fire, use only downed wood—see Tips—and bring some marshmallows!

Tips: If you want a campfire at Ranch Ponds bring some wood in case there is not enough downed wood nearby. Wood bundles can also be purchased at the Visitor Center. Look for the distinctive purple Pasqueflower in mid to late April.

Other options:

1. Golden Gate Kid's Programs. Check out the public programs run by Golden Gate State Park from Memorial Day to Labor Day. Education programs include a 'Kid's Hour' every Saturday as well as the popular evening campfire programs. For more information see www.parks.state.co.us. Campfire Programs are presented in the outdoor amphitheatre at Reverend's Ridge Campground during the summer.

2. Fish at Kriley Pond. Located 1.5 miles north of the Visitor Center next to Golden Gate Canyon Road, this deeper pond provides better fishing than Ranch Ponds and you'll often see people enjoying the easy roadside access. Enjoy the canyon breezes on a hot day, but note that this location is very exposed with no shelter from wind or sun. If you do stop here, make your way to the quieter side of the pond away from the road, or climb the small knoll behind for views.

3. Bike Ride to Ranch Ponds. Bike along the quiet Crawford Gulch Road on a 6 mile round trip (bike seat carrier and trailer combinations) from the Visitor Center to Ranch Ponds. The twisting canyon road passes original homesteads, old farm machinery and granite outcrops covered in orange lichen. It's a gentle downhill outward trip and then a steady climb for the return.

4. Snowshoe Hare Loop Trail. For those wanting a longer hike from Dude's Fishing Hole, continue down the valley on the Snowshoe Hare Trail through aspen groves and pine forest. The trail returns by climbing back up the hill past Rifleman Phillips Group Campground and then loops back to the east section of the Aspen Meadows Campground, roughly a 3 mile loop.

5. Enjoy Camping. Golden Gate State Park provides all sorts of choices from car camping, cabins and yurts open year round, to back country sites. Check at the visitor center, or on the web: www.parks.state.co.us for more information. The Reverend Ridge campground located near Panorama Point provides easy access car camping for first-time campers. The tent-only Aspen Meadow Camp ground provides a quieter 'get-away from it all', with access to a large grass meadow as well as Dude's Fishing Hole. Camping fees at this site are half price from Sunday through Thursday.

JEFFERSON COUNTY FAIRGROUND 14

Enjoy the playground with some more unusual structures that include balancing features and a rope wall. Explore the grounds on paved surfaces through a landscaped plaza and keep your eye out for any events—you might just stumble across a rodeo! You never know what you're going to find at the Fairgrounds.

Jefferson County Fairgrounds

15200 West 6th Avenue (at Indiana Street), Golden, CO 80401
303 271 6600
http://fairgrounds.jeffco.us

Open Hours: 7 days a week, 7am-10pm

Location: 5.3 miles from Golden Visitor Center.

Directions: Drive south on Washington for 0.6 miles. Turn right onto 19th Street. Go 0.5 miles to the stoplight at Hwy6. Turn left. Exit at Indiana Street. Turn right onto Indiana Street and then take the first right onto West 6th Avenue. Jefferson County Fairgrounds is signed from the Indiana Street exit. Turn left at the large electronic sign at the entrance into the Fairgrounds. For the playground, take the first right and follow this for 0.1 miles until you see the playground on your right.

Parking: Large paved parking lot adjacent to the playground and picnic area.

Season: All year. This site is exposed with little shelter. Avoid midday heat in summer and windy days in winter.

Restrooms: Fully equipped large restrooms with wheelchair access. These restrooms are immaculate and heated in winter!

Water: Drinking fountains in summer outside the restrooms and next to the playground (summer only).

Dogs: Yes. On-leash.

Jefferson County Fairgrounds is a large site that has undergone major refurbishments in the last 5 years. For those with young children it provides a great resource. The playground rarely has more than a handful of visitors and yet it has some unusual and fun features from its 2001 construction. Try the rope wall, or choose from a number of balancing options. Next to the playground there is a large group shelter with up to 40 picnic tables and adjacent grass areas for ball games and kite flying.

The Fairgrounds is a great place to bring bikes; smooth level paths circle the play area and shelter; good for trike riders and those just starting. The landscaped plaza area behind (west of) the Fairgrounds Office also provides some fun loops and combinations. This is a good point to visit the 4H office as well as the Fairgrounds Office and pick up brochures or ask about activities and events. In addition the large gravel parking lots are usually empty unless there is an event taking place, and these can be fun for your more able riders.

Inside the public arena

Explore the outdoor arenas and corrals on the Fairground. You may see a local rodeo, dog agility trials or horse training just by walking up, and unless it is posted, there is usually no charge. Under 5's can get a great glimpse of an activity they might not normally see. For any small horse enthusiasts, note that the Westernaires (a Jefferson County-based non profit organization that provides youth with training in western riding, precision drill and horse care) use the Fairgrounds as their training base. Every Saturday some of the 1000 plus team members are out practicing from 8am-5pm.

Other options:

1. Special Events. Plan your visit to coincide with a special event at the Fairgrounds. Visit the website http://jeffco.us/fair and look at the monthly events schedule. A great free event is the annual Jefferson County 4H fair. Held either the last weekend in July or first weekend in August, there are lots of farm animals to get close to, hands-on activities and things to make, as well as free horse rides.

2. Golden Heights Park. If you want a park that has slopes for winter sledding or have an able young skateboarder, visit nearby Golden Heights Park. The Park is located on West 2nd Avenue and Quaker Street; follow the 6th Avenue frontage road beyond the Fairgrounds to reach this site. In addition to the skateboard park, there is a small playground, grass fields, restrooms and a shelter. Be prepared for traffic noise; this park is right next to I70, and for this reason is not described in full.

3. Estates Park. Located just west of the Fairgrounds, at 16208 Ellsworth Drive. From the Indiana exit, follow West Ellsworth Avenue, turn right on McIntyre Circle and then immediately left on Ellsworth Drive. The park is on the north side of the road. Expect great views, lots of space, few people, a large playground, steep slopes that are good for winter sledding, and restrooms. A paved fitness loop encircles a tall grassland area. Follow dirt tracks through the grass to get away from the mown areas. The paved paths are generally good for bikes, but the fitness loop is too steep for the under 5's. The site is exposed to sun and wind.

Tips: Bring a bike or stroller and explore the Fairgrounds. This is good place for young bike riders. Don't be shy about wandering into the covered arena and checking out what's going on. You never know what you might see!

15 LIONS PARK

So many options from this location you'll have to come back for more. Play and paddle on a sandy beach alongside Clear Creek White Water Park, enjoy the lake and large playground in Lions Park or bike/stroll a 1 mile round trip on a secluded continuation of the Clear Creek Trail through lush cottonwood groves.

Lions Park, Clear Creek White Water Park, Clear Creek Trail to Terry Grant Park

1300 10th Street, Golden, CO 80401
City of Golden
303 384 8127
www.ci.golden.co.us

Location: 0.3 miles from Golden Visitor Center.

Directions: Turn left onto 10th Street and drive west 0.3 miles to reach parking on the left for Lions Park.

Parking: Large paved parking lot. If this is full, additional parking can be found at the following, all of which border the playground and grass area of Lions Park: 10th Street, Golden Community Center, Maple Street (opposite Lions Park entrance).

Season: All Year. Large cottonwood trees provide shade alongside the creek and in Lions Park. Great fall color on the Clear Creek Trail. In winter the trail only receives early morning sunshine and can be icy.

Restrooms: Fully equipped restrooms with wheelchair access are located at Lions Park parking lot and to the west side of the playground across the street (summer only).

Water: Drinking fountains are located outside the Lions Park restrooms and next to the Lions Park playground (summer only).

Dogs: Yes. On-leash. Look for the dog drinking fountain at the Lions Park playground. Dogs will enjoy the creek and especially the westwards continuation of the Clear Creek Trail.

Lions Park is Golden's showpiece park providing many options for play from a central area. Choose your activity according to the season and your interest.

In summer the emphasis is on keeping cool with shade, running water and creek side activities. West of the parking lot, Clear Creek Whitewater Park consists of 800 feet of carefully positioned boulders and rock bays that provide a challenging kayak park as well as lots of options for fishing, tubing, rock hopping, feet dipping and skipping stones. Shade can be found under the large cottonwoods at the west end of the kayak park.

Look for the small sandy beach adjacent to the Lions Park ball fields and parking lot; this can be a hit on a hot day with the kids. Sand has been added to the riverbank making a good place to build sand castles, splash in a shallow bay and watch the kayakers.

Across the road from Clear Creek the short grass, lake setting, tall cottonwoods and playground of Lions Park are popular year round. The play area consists of 2 large ramp and slide structures for different age groups, 4 tot swings, and 4 child swings. The play structures are set in a sand base and have ramp access. Bring sand digging toys. Other facilities near the playground include a shelter with picnic

tables, drinking fountain and sand volleyball pit. Tame resident Canada geese at the playground are loved by some, but not by others. Elsewhere picnic tables and barbecue grills are scattered under shade trees throughout Lions Park.

Contrast your trip to the Lions Park area by following a continuation of the Clear Creek Trail (at first on paved trail and then on a dirt/gravel track) to reach the trail end after 0.7 miles. Start opposite Lions Park and follow the trail westwards past a reservoir and under the large highway overpass. At this point the quiet and more secluded off-road section of the trail begins and takes you through tall woodland strewn with vines and ground cover and with plenty of opportunities for getting close to nature. The trail seems almost flat and works fine with strollers, though expect some bumps. Bicycles are permitted; bike seat carriers and trailer combinations are recommended unless your child is a good independent rider to cope with the stony trail. The trail ends where an irrigation ditch, Church Ditch, splits from the river in an area known as Terry Grant Park (managed by Jefferson County Open Space). Enjoy cool breezes and shade along this trail in the hot summer months.

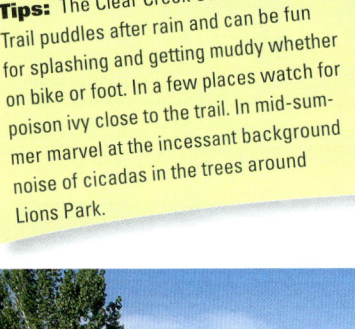

Tips: The Clear Creek Continuation Trail puddles after rain and can be fun for splashing and getting muddy whether on bike or foot. In a few places watch for poison ivy close to the trail. In mid-summer marvel at the incessant background noise of cicadas in the trees around Lions Park.

Clear Creek Continuation Trail to Terry Grant Park

Other options:

1. Special Events at Clear Creek White Water Park and Lions Park. Call Golden Visitor Center 303 279 3113 or visit the City of Golden website www.ci.golden.co.us for information on the Clear Creek White Water Festival in April, School of Mines Engineering Days the first Saturday in April (when cardboard rafts float down the kayak course), the Clear Creek White Water Festival in late May/early June, the Rocky Mountain Omnium cycle event on Memorial Day, the free Under 12's Fishing Derby in Lions Park the first Saturday in June, outdoor evening concerts and movies in the Park throughout the summer months and 4th of July celebrations with free fairground rides for kids, to name a few events.

2. Nearby Playgrounds. Lions Park is one of the most popular and heavily visited facilities in Golden. If you want to visit less busy parks with good playgrounds consider nearby: White Ash Mine Park, Norman D. Park and Beverly Heights Park—all within a mile distance—see separate guidebook entries.

3. Free Indoor Play. If you get stuck in the rain and still want to play, visit Golden Recreation Center's new free indoor play area, due to open in 2007. Go through the main entrance doors on the lower floor to access this area.

16 LOOKOUT MOUNTAIN NATURE CENTER

Touch a mountain lion paw, use binoculars, put on headphones and match wildlife sounds, see what animals like which wild flower plant, learn about dead trees and wild fires; it's hard to come away from Lookout Mountain Nature Center without having learnt something whatever the weather or season. Include a woodland or meadow loop hike or play on boulders.

Lookout Mountain Nature Center and Preserve

910 Colorow Road, Golden, Colorado 80401
Jefferson County Open Space
303 526 0594
www.openspace.jeffco.us

Open Hours: Nature Center: Tuesday – Sunday 10am-4pm. Lookout Mountain Preserve: 8am-dusk, daily

Location: 7.1 miles from Golden Visitor Center.

Directions: Drive south on Washington for 0.6 miles. Turn right onto 19th Street. Go 0.5 miles to the stoplight on Hwy6. 19th turns into Lookout Mountain Road. Follow this past switchbacks and turn right onto Colorow Road just after Buffalo Bill's Lookout and Museum. Lookout Mountain Nature Center is signed at this point; turn left after 0.7 miles through large metal gates into the Nature Center.

Parking: large paved parking lot in the Nature Center grounds.

Season: All year. There's something different to see with every season (and good piles of snow in the winter).

Restrooms: Fully equipped restrooms with wheelchair access are available inside the Nature Center (follow the mule deer tracks in the tiled floor). When the Center is closed, but the Preserve is open, an external door gives access to the same facility.

Water: Drinking fountains inside the Center. Bring water when the Center is closed.

Dogs: No.

Formerly owned by the Denver entrepreneur, Charles Boettcher, this 110-acre family estate is now known as Lookout Mountain Nature Center and Preserve. Tailor your trip for inside and outside activities with choices from 'touch and feel' exhibits, a story room with nature books, exploring the loop trails, looking for signs of nature (pick up a handout), and following interpretative trails themed on wild plants and the Ponderosa Pine Forest.

Outside: The Preserve has two hiking loops on gentle trails. The slightly longer (1.4 mile round trip from the parking lot) Meadow Loop Trail is best for children in backpacks or more able hikers. In late summer the tall grass sections of the trail tower over kid's heads and are alive with jumping grasshoppers. The Forest Loop of 0.6 miles is a great length for your 3 year olds and takes you across bridges and through Ponderosa Pine Forest. This trail can also be managed with any type of stroller although expect some bumps. Listen for the chatter of the black Abert's squirrel and look for fragments of nibbled pinecones. At the end of both loops on the west side of Boettcher mansion, look for the little stone pavilion with seats and a fireplace. Children love this place for a picnic and peek-a-boo games.

Looking for ants - Toddler Times Program

Around the outside of the Nature Center building there is a signed wild plant trail—wheelchair accessible. There are also many benches and picnic tables in shaded areas.

Inside: Lookout Mountain Nature Center was built in 1997 and is 'state-of-the-art' for its energy saving design and construction. Look for floors made from recycled boxcars, decking from recycled plastic bottles and tiling from old car windshields.

Inside the Center there are plenty of things to touch, feel and move next to a life-size mountain lion, black bear and other animals. A separate 'Observation Area' is always popular, with binoculars and headphones to watch and listen for wildlife, and tips for young naturalists (and parents!) on how to do this. If you have the inclination, don't forget the reading room with cushions and large books on nature, or bring a book of your own.

In the parking lot there are some large boulders at the north end, which are fun for scrambling around. Look for lichens and moss in the crevices. In winter, pack snow boots for kids to climb over the piles of snow remaining from snow clearance operations.

Tips: Bring a picnic. Pack plenty of clothing that can be layered on and off; the temperatures differ from Golden, which is 2000 feet lower elevation. Inside the Center save some change for the Abert's squirrel donation box. Place a coin in the box hear the squirrel chatter!

Other options:

1. Buffalo Bill Museum and Grave (and Cafe!) Return down Lookout Mountain Road to Buffalo Bill Museum and Grave. At the overlook, there are great views of Golden, Denver, and the eastern plains, and you can use an in-situ viewer for a quarter. The nearby café provides eats and treats as well as an extensive gift shop, which may or may not be advisable to visit with an under 5. A short paved walk leads to Buffalo Bill's grave. There is some brief information about Buffalo Bill posted outside the café if a museum trip doesn't appeal. The cafe has wonderful fudge! Alternatively, for under 5's happy to sit in backpacks you can walk a 1 mile open space trail from the Nature Center to the same location. Start at the pullout on Colorow Road just opposite the entrance gates to Lookout Mountain Nature Center; look for trailhead signs and a path descending towards a saddle.

2. Toddler Times Program. Time your visit to coincide with a Toddler Times program aimed at children ages 2-5. The programs are free and run monthly with weekend and midweek morning start times. Each program has a special theme tied in with the season and kids will learn, feel, see, and do an activity with a craft to take home. Great staff put a huge amount of effort into these programs. Call 720 497 7600 for more information or to request a quarterly brochure. This information is also on the web site under Lookout Mountain Nature Center—Public Programs: www.openspace.jeffco.us. Also check their schedule for additional family programs and activities held at different Jefferson County Open Space locations every month.

N. TABLE MOUNTAIN QUARRY

17

North Table Mountain Quarry and Pond

Wyoming Circle and Pine View Road, Golden, CO 80403
Jefferson County Open Space and City of Golden
303 384 8127
www.ci.golden.co.us/

Location: 1.9 miles from Golden Visitor Center.

Directions: Drive west on 10th Street. Turn left onto Ford Street and follow this north to its end at 1.7 miles. Turn right at the stop sign onto Pine Ridge Road and then an immediate left onto Wyoming Circle. This road curves to the left. After 0.1 miles turn left into the parking lot with the sign 'North Table Mountain Trailhead' opposite Pine View Road.

Parking: 20 vehicle spaces on a paved parking lot.

Season: All year. This is an exposed hike with no shelter. Avoid midday heat in summer, cold windy days in winter and being caught in thunderstorms. The mud base trails can be very 'sticky' up to 48 hours after heavy rain.

Restrooms: No.

Water: No. Bring plenty of water especially in summer.

Dogs: Yes. On-leash.

Hike to the top of North Table Mountain and explore a quarry and an adventurous loop trail round the quarry perimeter, or travel further to scramble over rocks or look for wildlife at a hidden pond. All this is set within 1,945-acres of Open Space—grasslands, lichen rock gardens, and cliff habitat on a 63 million year old volcanic plateau.

This trailhead accesses well-used trails and a quarry at the north end of North Table Mountain. Having hiked to the Mesa plateau, explore the large old quarry, try an adventurous loop trail around its perimeter, or continue hiking eastwards to a wildlife pond. This hike will suit your more able young hiker, or infants and toddlers in backpacks. Although the approach can be slightly long for small children, coax them along because there are many opportunities for play and looking at nature. A surprising number of family groups use this trail, testifying to its popularity. North Table Mountain may see changes in trails and access under the new Jefferson County Park Management Plan. Watch for new signs at the trailhead and on trails.

Hiking directions: From the trailhead, follow the trail behind the houses until it merges with a dirt maintenance track leading to a water tower. Pass this and follow a foot track up the hill on its south side before linking in with another gravel access road bordered by a chain link fence (0.3 miles). Continue up this track until you arrive at the former Lafarge quarry site and the plateau of the Mesa.

Explore the 'lunar-landscape' of the quarry and climb a child-size mountain of gravel on its east side. To do the loop round the quarry, look for a well defined vehicle track on the northeast side and follow this round its east edge, until you split off on a smaller trail at its south end. The trail narrows between drop offs on its western side, which is an exciting and dramatic adventure for the young, but

Tips: Bring a walking stick or hiking pole for young hikers; it may make the steep section more fun. Bring food and water. You may also be lucky to catch a glimpse, or hear the cries, of Prairie Falcons, which nest further along the cliffs from early January.

Other options:

1. Climb to the Summit of North Table Mountain 6566 feet. To the north of the wildlife pond you can see a prominent rock pinnacle. For the extra adventurous in your group it is a short distance to these rock outcrops. Easy scrambling gives access to the top and a sense of achievement to your summiting under 5. Take care over loose rock and practice Leave No Trace ethics by walking on hard surfaces to avoid crushing plants; vegetation grows very slowly under these harsh rocky conditions.

watch your kids at this point. The trail continues around the quarry, although more faintly, until you descend a narrow mini-ridge at its north point bringing you back to the start. As you walk, look for lichen gardens and wild flowers and keep an eye out for ravens, which regularly circle this area and play on the updrafts from the cliffs.

If you choose to go to the wildlife pond, take the gravel vehicle track eastwards until the trail splits at 0.8 miles. Look left and 50 yards north from the track you'll see an earth embankment with the pond behind. The water level fluctuates with the season. In summer look for water skippers and dragonflies around the cattails. In winter you may get a glimpse of the 80-100 mule deer that use this area, or prairie dogs in the distance. Enjoy the rocky foreshore, but walk with care avoiding small plants or lichens. From this point there are good views towards Denver.

NORMAN D. MEMORIAL PARK 18

A great little park to escape the summer heat with plenty of tall tree shade (even on the playground!) and grass areas to spread out. Balance on the playground's long metal tube, find a great tree to climb and crawl through the concrete tunnel. Explore Tucker Gulch stream and look for bugs either in the park or along the continuation multiuse trail to the east.

Norman D. Memorial Park and Tucker Gulch

North Ford Street, Golden CO 80403
City of Golden
303 384 8127
www.ci.golden.co.us

Location: 1.1 miles from Golden Visitor Center.

Directions: Go east on 10th Street. Turn left on Ford Street to reach Norman D. Memorial Park on your left at 1 mile, just before the right turn for Mesa Drive.

Parking: 9 vehicle spaces in a paved off-road parking lot. If this is full, (unlikely unless there is a group booking at the shelters) park in nearby residential streets.

Restrooms: Port-a-potty restroom—no wheelchair access.

Water: Yes. Drinking fountain due to be installed next to the shelters (summer only).

Dogs: Yes. On-leash.

Norman D. Memorial Park has a quiet charm. It is rare to find more than a couple of cars in the parking lot and its location next to Tucker Gulch makes its boundary a wildlife haven, with trees alive with territorial robins in early spring.

The playground is at the west end of the park, set back at least 150 yards from the road. Facilities include a large ramp and slide, 2 tot swings and an unusually long bouncy pipe. There is good tree climbing and potential for 'dens' nearby. Adjacent to the play area there is a large grass area suitable for ball games. Other facilities in this park include 2 new shelters with picnic tables.

In the central section of the park there is a half-submerged section of large concrete pipe. This may look ugly but with surrounding low stone walls, a sunken grass area and large trees, it attracts children like a magnet. In the fall, look for the rattling seedpods scattered around the base of the honey locust tree.

The north side of the park is bordered by Tucker Gulch stream. There isn't always water in the Gulch, but in spring/early summer there is usually a reasonable flow and the vegetation can be lush. Scramble down the bank to explore and cool off hot feet.

The recent housing development on the west boundary of the park will lead to some changes in the park. A paved multi-use bike trail will connect the park from Tucker Gulch Trail to the east, past the playground and link with the new housing and the east end of Golden Gate Canyon Road. Previously there was no paved access to the playground and the approach was over grass.

Tips: Bring old shoes that can get wet for exploring the Gulch. Bring a clear plastic container with lid for looking at insects from the grass or creek. Visit the Gulch after heavy rainfall and enjoy watching it turn from a sluggish stream to a faster flowing creek.

At the spillway on Tucker Gulch Trail

Other options:

1. Tucker Gulch Bike Trail going east. Tucker Gulch Trail provides more stream exploration options just 5mins from the park. The paved trail starts opposite the parking lot on the east side of North Ford Street and is clearly marked. Follow the trail downstream for less than 5mins to reach an area of large cottonwoods with a concrete spillway on your left. The spillway (always low flow except after heavy rainfall) provides a great place for playing in the stream. Wade, ride a bike across it, or watch sticks or leaves flow over the spillway. Walk a further 50 yards down the trail and you reach a shaded picnic table. From here access the stream and a stony beach. The trail distance to this point is about 0.2 miles and can be good riding for your more able bike riders, although they may need a push back up the hill for the return journey.

2. Tucker Gulch Bike Trail going west. Follow the new stretch of multi-use bike trail (completion due 2006/7) out of the park westwards for something to eat or drink. The trail will then parallel Hwy93 and link through to the Canyon Point Mall for bagels, coffee and sandwiches and where you can find the kid-friendly Ali Baba restaurant.

NORTH GOLDEN BIKE LOOP 19

Make a tour of North Golden on multi-use trails and get to know its neighborhoods and geography. Parents get a work out on the steep section, whether on a bike or pushing a jogging stroller, while kids have at least 4 fun stopping points. Choose from 4 City of Golden parks and play areas, or look for wildlife along Tucker Gulch on the downhill cruise back to Downtown Golden.

North Golden Loop Bike Trail

Extends north of Lions Park for the equivalent of 10 blocks, then 4 blocks east followed by the return leg back to 10th Street.
City of Golden
303 384 8127
www.ci.golden.co.us/

Location: 0.3 miles from Golden Visitor Center.

Directions: Turn left onto 10th Street and drive 0.3 miles west to reach parking on the left for Lions Park.

Parking: Large paved parking lot. If this is full, additional parking can be found at the following, all of which border the playground and grass area of the park: 10th Street, Golden Recreation Center, Maple Street (opposite Lions Park entrance).

Season: All year. The City of Golden maintains its paved multi-use trails and keeps them snow-free throughout the year. Avoid summer midday heat.

Restrooms: Fully equipped restrooms at Lions Park parking lot and to the west side of the Lions Park playground (summer only).

Water: Drinking fountains at Lions Park parking lot and Lions Park playground (summer only).

Dogs: Yes. On-leash. Dog drinking fountains at New Loveland Mine Park and Lions Park playground.

Alternative Start Point—New Loveland Mine Park on 5th Street; An alternative start point for the bike trail, which is both quiet and scenic, places you up the hill and north of Lions Park at New Loveland Mine Park. This small parking lot always has space, and comes with a port-a-potty restroom. Follow the bike loop described for Lions Park if you start here.

Directions: Drive north on Washington Avenue and turn left onto 5th Street at 0.3 miles. Follow this west for several blocks until just before its end at the junction with Rubey Drive (0.7 miles). The parking lot is signed on the left side of the road, adjacent to the bike trail and play area.

Distance: 3.5 mile paved loop, 0.4 miles on street. This beautiful trail gives a scenic and varied tour of the north part of Golden. By incorporating 4 very different parks and 2 creek-side trails, users can plan for just the length and style of outing they want. Because of the one steep climb on this loop, this trip is recommended for bike seat carriers, trailer combinations or strollers. Even if you have a very able young rider and are willing to give them a push, the gradients and distance may make this unsuitable for independent wheeling.

The trail is described clockwise from Lions Park. It includes one steep gradient rising from Lions

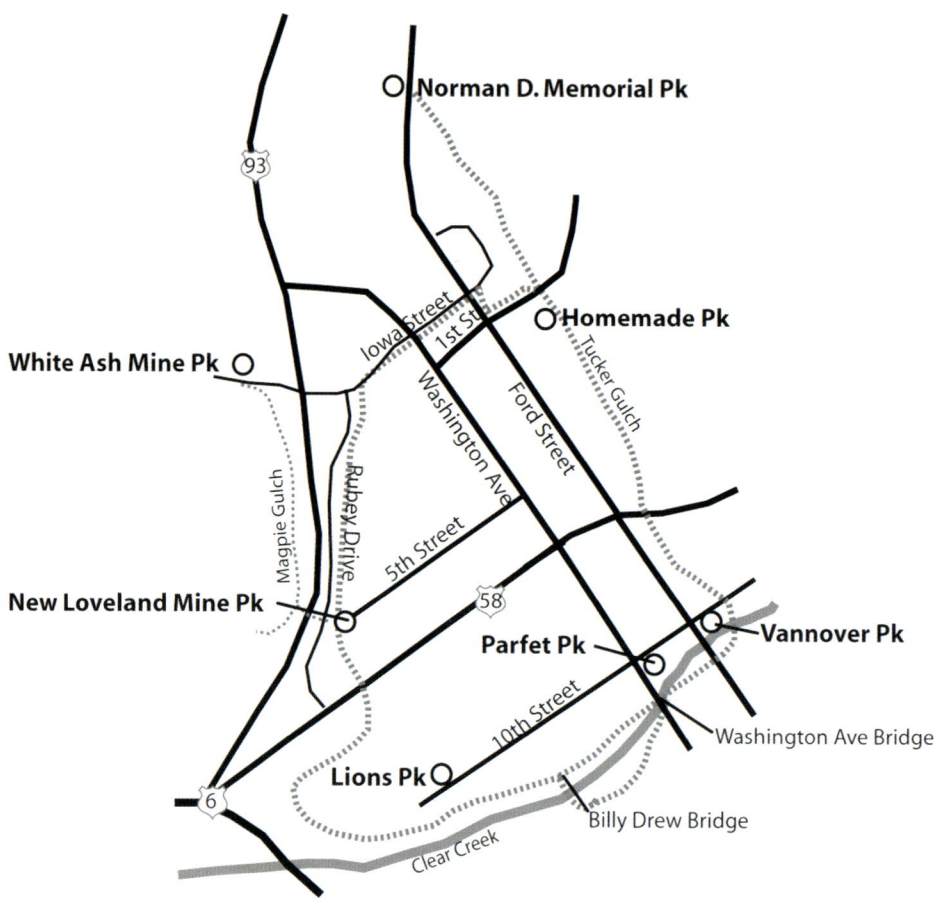

Park to New Loveland Mine Park and 0.4 miles of fairly quiet streets to complete the 'loop'. The loop is described so that users complete the steep section first and then follow gentle gradients and downhill for the rest of the loop.

Start at Lions Park. Follow the Clear Creek Trail west past City of Golden RV Park and reservoir. The trail leaves Clear Creek at the reservoir and climbs via a series of bends, over CO58 by a footbridge, and emerges in the large open space area of New Loveland Mine Park. Exit New Loveland Mine Park at its north end and take the large sidewalk on Rubey Drive to its end at Iowa Street. Turn right (east) onto Iowa and follow it across the stoplight at Washington Avenue to its end at Ford Street. Turn right (south), and then take the first left onto First Street, and go down the steep hill. At the bottom of the hill, Tucker Gulch stream and its paved off-road trail are visible. Join the Tucker Gulch trail just below the bridge and follow this south, first over a small concrete bridge, and then over several small wooden bridges. Cross over 7th Street, follow the trail under CO58, cross over 10th, and emerge in Vanover Park next to Clear Creek. Follow the trail rightwards (west) using the underpass at Ford Street and parallel Clear Creek to reach Washington Bridge. Either stop here and cross the bridge to reach Parfet Park or continue on the south side of the creek past Clear Creek History Park. Turn right at the end of the History Park over Billy Drew footbridge to rejoin Clear Creek Trail. Follow this west past White Water Kayak Park until you arrive opposite Lions Park.

Stop wherever you wish on the 3.5 mile trail, but the most logical play places are New Loveland Mine Park, Tucker Gulch and Vanover Park described below:

New Loveland Mine Park

Tips: Go bug hunting along Tucker Gulch in the stream or grassland; bring a plastic pot with lid and a magnifying glass. The little concrete foot bridge just south of First Street makes a good point to start exploring. Bring a snack for one of the parks along the bike trail.

Other options:

1. North section of Tucker Gulch Trail and Norman D. Memorial Park. When the bike loop joins the Tucker Gulch Trail instead of turning south (downhill), explore the remaining north portion of the trail. This follows the Gulch for 0.4 miles before ending at Ford Street and opposite Norman D. Memorial Park (pg 141).

2. White Ash Mine Park detour. Opposite Mitchell Elementary School on Rubey Drive, a footbridge leads over Hwy93 to Magpie Gulch. Turn right (north) over the bridge and follow the trail a short distance until it emerges on Iowa Street. Turn left on Iowa Street and then take the first right onto White Ash Drive. This brings you immediately to the park of the same name on the right (pg 156).

20 NREL

Did you know that the first solar cells were used to power space satellites? Learn about the cars of the future, flip the 'sun' switch and power the ski lift, or get up close to solar panels and wind turbines. There's plenty to look at and touch in the exhibit hall. If you have the energy, take an exploratory hike up the NREL Easement Trail to South Table Mountain, or climb over the pirate boat at nearby Tanglewood Playground.

National Renewable Energy Laboratory Visitor Center

15013 Denver West Parkway, Golden, CO 80401
303 384 6565
www.nrel.gov/visitors_center/

Open Hours: 9am-5pm. Monday through Friday. Closed on weekends and major holidays.
Location: 5 miles from Golden Visitor Center.
Directions: Drive west on 10th Street. Turn right onto Ford Street and follow this road as it turns into Jackson Street and then South Golden Road. Just after South Golden Road goes under I 70, at about 3.8 miles, turn left. This is still a continuation of South Golden Road. Follow this road through the Mall and across several 4-way stops to the stoplight with Denver West Parkway. Turn left onto Denver West Parkway and drive over I70 to the third stoplight. Turn left onto a continuation of Denver West Parkway (the Denver West Marriott Hotel is on the left corner of the stoplight). Follow the Parkway road to its end at the NREL Visitor Center.
Parking: Large paved parking lot.
Season: All year. Avoid summer midday heat.
Restrooms: Fully equipped restrooms with wheelchair access inside the Visitor Center.
Water: Drinking Fountains inside the Visitor Center.
Dogs: No in the Visitor Center, but yes on the NREL Easement Open Space Trail on-leash.

A visit to the NREL Visitor Center will give any young person a taste of what renewable energy and solar power is all about—and this can be taken to the simplest level. The Visitor Center has exhibits both inside and out, providing an experience that will suit all ages. While the Center may not sustain a particularly long visit for the under 5's, it's another great example of a free learning resource on the Front Range. If you live locally, you may want to visit on a regular basis as the kids get older and can grasp the more complex concepts on display. Don't forget to check out the shelves and brochure racks filled with information on renewable energy and other topics, ranging from teaching materials through to homeowner advice.

The compact energy saving visitor building is scenically located next to 175-acres of grassland open space. As you walk up to the entrance past a shaded walk with native plants, see the examples of road signs powered by solar energy. Inside, take a self-guided tour and pick an exhibit that attracts your

Tanglewood Park

Tips: Finding NREL can be a little complicated. If you are having problems, either locating the Visitor Center or the NREL Conservation Easement Trailhead for South Table Mountain, search on the following web sites for maps and more information: www.nrel.gov/visitors_center/ and www.tablemountains.org/Pages/Maps+Trails/stmtrails.htm

Solar powered pond pump

Other options:

1. Hike up South Table Mountain—south end. Take a hike, part or all of the way, to South Table Mountain plateau through 175 acres of Jefferson County Open Space (prairie grasslands and wet gulch). This will suit your more able hikers, or bring a backpack for infants and toddlers. This trail is not suitable for strollers. Caution: South Table Mountain trailheads are in rattle-snake country—in summer watch out and listen on trails. The trailhead is at the south end of the parking lot. After half a mile, the approach trail splits; either path will take you to the top of South Table Mountain and you can make a 2 mile loop outing from this point. Take plenty of water.

2. Tanglewood Sports Park and Playground—13725 Denver West Circle. For a playground outing close to Denver West Village and Colorado Mills, try the popular Tanglewood Park. Enjoy a large pirate boat sunk in a sand base, tot and child swings and a larger than average (and with more climbing fun) ramp and slide structure. Other facilities include restrooms (fully equipped), drinking fountains, picnic tables and shelters. From NREL drive across the Denver Marriot Hotel stoplight on Denver West Parkway, Tanglewood Park is about half a mile on your left with a 90 vehicle space paved parking lot.

youngster—you can turn a handle to see how much more energy it takes to power a regular everyday light bulb compared to an energy saving bulb—or see the hydrogen cars of the future. This may all be above the youngest visitors, but there's still plenty to look at and touch. Outside the Center there are places to run and picnic, surrounded by examples of solar roof panels on small sheds. A small gravel path leads back to the parking lot.

21 PROSPECT PARK

Don't miss Prospect Park. Set back from roads and located next to Clear Creek you can enjoy fishing, wading, bird-watching, biking, woodland trails, exploration and a choice of 2 playgrounds all within 50 yards of a parking lot that's usually empty mid-week.

Prospect Park and Wheat Ridge Green Belt

11300 West 44th Avenue, Wheat Ridge 80033
City of Wheat Ridge
303 234 5900
www.ci.wheatridge.co.us

Location: 5.5 miles from Golden Visitor Center.

Directions: Drive east on 10th Street (which turns into West 44th Avenue). Continue on this road, which goes under I70, through three stoplights. Look for Prospect RV Park on your right at 5.3 miles. Turn right into Prospect Park at 5.5 miles. Look for the brown entrance sign.

Parking: There are several parking options, but the best point for accessing Clear Creek and the playgrounds is at the south end of the site. Follow the entrance road for 0.4 miles as it curves to the east around Prospect Lake ending at a large paved parking lot for about 80 cars.

Season: All year. Attractive spring foliage, summer shade and great fall color from the large cottonwoods.

Restrooms: Fully equipped restrooms with wheelchair access at the south end parking lot.

Water: Drinking fountains are located outside the restrooms, and next to the west playground (summer only).

Dogs: Yes. On-leash.

It would be easy to miss Prospect Park with its minimal signage, yet those who persevere are rewarded with a regionally significant park with a wealth of recreation opportunities. The park is located next to Clear Creek, intersected by the multi-use Clear Creek Trail, and contains the fairly large Prospect Lake. In addition, gravel-base trails through old woodland link to other lakes and wetland areas along the 250-acre Wheatridge Greenbelt Open Space Corridor. Pick up a map at the information kiosk in the parking lot to get your bearings.

The most kid-friendly attractions are the 2 playgrounds with different play structures, the large lake with wheelchair/stroller access to a fishing jetty, easy river access for wading and wilder woodland areas for exploring and looking at nature. Prospect Lake also has resident and migratory duck and geese populations which means you can guarantee seeing birds up close.

Use this park as a base for your favorite activity. The multi-use paved Clear Creek Trail provides options for young bike riders, or doing a section of the trail with a jogging stroller. The no bike access trails on the south side of the river are accessible with strollers and allow exploration of the woodland. Of the 2 playgrounds, the west site has some fun and unusual climbing and balance structures and gives closest access to the lake and fishing jetty. In addition there are grass areas for ball games, a Habitat Garden planted with native shrubs, and a small shelter with picnic tables. The east site has new 2006 playground equipment, which is also large and fun, and gives closest access to the foot bridge, group shelters and picnic tables.

Tips: Bring some binoculars for bird watching, a plastic container to look at bugs from the river, and a fishing rod. Note: If the large shelter has a group booking on a summer weekend afternoon, this normally quiet park can be very busy with difficult parking. Caution: Be aware of patches of poison ivy growing next to the woodland trails on the south side of the river.

East playground

Other options:

1. Wheatridge Greenbelt Conservation Area. Walk or take a stroller across the creek and into the woodland of Wheatridge Greenbelt Conservation Area. From the foot bridge take a loop-hiking trail on crushed gravel under mature cottonwoods. A right turn (west) leads to Bass and West Lakes within half a mile. A left turn (east) follows a loop walk of under a mile round trip.

2. Clear Creek Trail. Explore sections of the Clear Creek Trail by bicycle. From the parking lot either go west and reach Tabor Lake in a quarter of a mile, or go east and reach Anderson Park (about 1.5 miles) and Johnson Park (about 2.5 miles), each located next to Clear Creek with a playground, fully equipped restrooms and picnic areas.

22 TONY GRAMPSAS

One of the few playgrounds in Golden with a tire swing, and the bonus of an off-leash dog park, set well away from the parking lot down a no outlet road. Quiet midweek, shaded, and with lots of grass space, this is a good summer outing. Contrast the park experience with a walk along the wilder Fire Crusher Trail where you can play in the woods, climb trees and look for hedgerow apples in a lush setting.

Tony Grampsas Memorial Sports Complex and Fire Crusher Trail

44th and Salvia, Golden CO 80401
City of Golden
303 384 8127
www.ci.golden.co.us

Location: 2.4 miles from Golden Visitor Center.

Directions: Drive east on 10th Street (which turns into West 44th Avenue) for 1.9 miles. Shortly after Colorado Railroad Museum, you will see the sign for Tony Grampsas Park. Turn left onto Salvia Street. Follow this No Outlet road (past Compass Montessori School on your left) to the parking lot at its end.

Parking: Park at the east end of the large gravel parking lot for closest access to paved trails leading to the playground.

Season: All year. Good shade from cottonwoods in summer.

Restrooms: 4 vault restrooms with wheelchair access.

Water: Drinking fountain and faucet located on the north side of the shelter (summer only).

Dogs: Yes. On-leash except inside the Dog Park located at the far north end of the park.

Dedicated to Tony Grampsas, a former Coors employee and a friend of Parks and Recreation in the State Legislature, this 63-acre park was opened in 2000. At first glance this park with 3 ball fields might not appeal to kids, and it would be easy to miss the playground. However, tucked away at the southeast corner of North Table Mountain and bordered by Jefferson County Open Space and a private reservoir it can be a quiet and peaceful outing. Equipped for large-scale use on the weekends, avoid these and enjoy Tony Grampsas on a quiet morning.

The small playground is set back from the parking lot along a paved trail so you should have no concerns about moving cars. Facilities include a ramp and slide structure and a tire swing; this alone will be exciting enough for the kids to make the trip worthwhile. The play area is surrounded by level paved trails—good for just-starting bike and trike riders. As you play at the park don't be put off by the strange stuffed animals behind the play area. This is a fenced target practice area for Golden High Country Archers who quietly go about their business with bow and arrow. Watch through the fence if you are interested.

Other facilities include 4 large shelters and grills for group reservation, 3 horseshoe pits and sand volleyball. In summer the grass irrigation systems send 50 foot jets of water across soft green grass. Dodge around them for a fun and cooling diversion.

Off-leash in the Dog Park

Fire Crusher Trail

Tips: Don't miss exploring the wooded Fire Crusher Trail to the north of Tony Grampsas Park. In late spring the nearby Church Ditch flows swiftly with irrigation water and the scent from honey locust blossom fills the air. In the fall, look for the small green 'hedgerow apples' of the Osage Orange shrub on the ground. Squirrels love them, the seeds are edible and the skin of a ripe fruit has an orange-peel smell. Bring bikes/trikes for the paved paths around the Tony Grampsas.

Other options:

1. Fire Crusher Trail. Take a great little 0.3 mile mini-hike over a wooden bridge and then along an easy wooded trail to access Tony Grampsas Park. Dense thickets of Osage Orange border the trail and Church Ditch, indicating a link to the past; settlers planted this shrub to make a livestock-proof natural fence in the days before barbed wire. Find trees to climb and explore the woodland along the trail.

Directions: Park on the south side of Easley Road on the road shoulder under a large cottonwood tree (space for about 5 vehicles). The pullout is located 0.7 miles down Easley Road from the Easley Way/Easley Road junction. Look for pedestrian crossing signs. From the parking area cross a small wooden bridge over the ditch and turn right (west) at the City of Golden Trailhead sign. Follow this until you are under a large group of honey locust trees from where the tennis courts and playground of Tony Grampsas Park can be seen. The entire Fire Crusher Trail spans 1.3 miles from the east side of the Tony Grampsas Gym on Salvia Street (look for the trailhead sign), then parallels Easley Road next to the rushing waters (seasonal) of Church Ditch, before skirting around the dog park and ending on West 50th Avenue and Quaker Street. From here it is just two blocks to Fairmount Park (pg 119).

2. Fairmount Trail. This newly designated 3 mile trail contours around the base of North Table Mountain on its east side to link with Arvada Blunn Reservoir (pg 96) on West 64th Parkway. Start opposite the Easley Road parking area described for Fire Crusher Trail above and look for the information board. In summer the rabbit brush and sage vegetation is alive with grasshoppers. The narrow, unpaved multi-use trail follows irrigation ditch right-of-way land and passes through developed residential areas.

3. Colorado Railroad Museum located a hop and a skipaway (0.2 miles pg 109).

The dog park is located at the north end of the park past the ball fields. Follow a paved path through the double-gated entrance where the pavement ends at a level area and picnic table. The fenced site is shaded with cottonwoods and native shrubs set against a slope. Pet pick-up bags and a disposal bin are provided at the entrance.

23 TRICERATOPS TRAIL

See Triceratops dinosaur tracks up close by following a cleverly sculpted trail through a former clay-mining pit. Look for traces of the area's mining past between vertical fins of rock set against a backdrop of old dragline machines and views of the North and South Table Mesas. Follow your visit by climbing on top of a 15 foot dinosaur, excavating for bones and picnicking at nearby Discovery Park.

Triceratops Trail on Parfet Prehistoric Preserve

Located on the east side of Hwy6 and the north end of Fossil Trace Golf Course.
Golden CO 80401
Friends of Dinosaur Ridge
303 697 3466
www.dinoridge.org

Trail distance: 1.25 miles round trip.
Location: 1 mile from Golden Visitor Center
Directions: Drive south on Washington for 0.6 miles. Turn right onto19th Street. Turn left onto Jones Road (immediately after the car dealership 'Stevinson Golden Ford'). Look for signs marked 'Triceratops Trail'. Follow Jones Road (gravel) to its end behind the apartment building and adjacent to the bike trail on Hwy6.
Parking: Use the (6) designated parking spaces marked 'Triceratops Trail'. If this parking area is full (unlikely) return to 19th street and look for nearby parking in adjacent streets.
Season: All year. There is little shade—avoid midday summer heat.
Restrooms: No.
Water: No. Bring water.
Dogs: Yes. On-leash.

There are few places where you can see well-preserved dinosaur tracks really close, but this is one of them. Triceratops Trail is a recent addition to the opportunities to look for fossils and dinosaur footprints around the Golden area. Combined with the old mining machinery you can see from the trail, and the unusual ups and downs as the trail twists through the old clay workings, this location makes a great outing with kids.

Triceratops Trail can be done on foot, on bike by your more able young bikers (they will need some help here and there) and strollers. The trail has a gravel base and some bumps to negotiate but all are manageable. Native grasses and shrubs border the trail and from its elevated position you have great views towards Golden and over Fossil Trace Golf Course. Caution: There are some steep drops away from the trail, but fencing and barriers where it is most needed. Keep your eye on unsteady toddlers!

Formerly mined for clay for five generations, what had become redundant land was reclaimed for housing, and the golf course was opened in 2004. With the discovery of significant fossil traces during development there was great public concern for their protection. Two years later thanks to the owners the Parfet family, Friends of Dinosaur Ridge, and enthusiasts in the local community,

Triceratops Trail was opened to the public.

From the parking lot turn left (south) onto the paved multiuse trail paralleling Hwy6. The trail immediately takes you through a gulch with large cottonwoods. After approximately 300 yards look for signs to the start of the Triceratops Trail on your left. Pick up a guide in the brochure box at the start. This, together with interpretive signs along the route, explains the history and geology of the area with special focus on the Triceratops dinosaur.

Kids will be excited at the first fossil site, where a steep zigzag track leads down into a clay cutting to access a viewing platform. At other points you can also see how miners dug the clay out by shovel between the vertical sandstone walls and used logs to brace the sides. If the sandstone walls were starting to shift the "singing log" would creak and hum. Some of the best fossils are found towards the end of the trail with large clear Triceratops tracks and palm fronds preserved from a sub-tropical swamp.

The trail ends at 0.6 miles where a fence separates the public access area from the golf course. Retrace your steps for the return journey.

Discovery Park

154 ♦ TRICERATOPS TRAIL

Tips: Does your child like cranes or construction? Bring a matchbox truck or equivalent and let them dig with it in one of the small piles of clay alongside the Triceratops Trail. You can help them pick up on the theme of the clay mining by pointing out the old dragline machines that can be seen from the trail.

Discovery Park

Other options:

1. Discovery Park. This compact and unusual 2006 park picks up on the theme of the nearby Triceratops Trail. You can climb all over and under a dinosaur as well as excavate for 'skeletons' in sand. There is also a small climbing wall, giant turtle and grass maze. Facilities include a small shelter, picnic tables, and a drinking fountain for people and dogs (summer only). There are no restrooms. To get to this park drive 0.4 miles south along Illinois Street from the stoplight on 19th Street. Park on Illinois Street.

2. Letterboxing. The Triceratops Trail is also a Letterbox site where a set of clues lead to a hidden box with a stamp in it. See www.letterboxing.org

3. Fossil Trace Golf Course. A life-size Triceratops skull replica and exhibits on the prehistoric plants and dinosaurs of this area can be seen at the Fossil Trace Club House. The clubhouse is located to the north. Turn left from Hwy6 into Jefferson County Parkway, and then take the first left onto Illinois Street and follow signs.

24 WHITE ASH MINE PARK ....

A true playground outing, particularly good for young bike riders, kite flying and winter warmth. Hunt for bugs in the unmown grassland adjacent to the trails and look at different grasses and wildflowers. Located just off Hwy93 on the north side of Golden, this park is easily found and makes a good meeting-up point.

White Ash Mine Park

White Ash Drive, Golden, CO 80403
City of Golden
303 384 8127
www.ci.golden.co.us

Location: 1 mile from Golden Visitor Center.

Directions: Drive north on Washington Avenue. Turn left at the stoplight onto Iowa Street. Follow Iowa Street straight over the stoplight on Hwy93 and turn right onto White Ash Drive. The park is immediately on the right.

Parking: There are 2 designated parking spaces at this entrance; 2 are for accessible parking. There is plenty of parking on the residential street White Ash Drive. Additional designated parking can be found to the north further up White Ash Drive, but this takes you further away from the playground, and is less helpful if you have small children.

Season: All year. This site is exposed with little shade and can be hot in summer. Avoid midday sun in summer and cold windy days in winter.

Restrooms: Port-a-potty restroom with no wheelchair access.

Water: Drinking fountain on the north side of the playground (summer only).

Dogs: Yes. On-leash.

T he playground and open space at White Ash Mine Park (the name reflects Golden's coal mining history of the 1880's and 90's) is spacious and smart, reflecting its role as a planned recreational facility within the surrounding housing development. Due to its relatively recent construction (1998) the site lacks mature trees and can be very exposed, but this also makes it warm and sunny on windless winter days and great for kite flying. The playground has 2 ramp and slide structures, 4 child swings and 2 tot swings. Other facilities next to the playground include a shelter and picnic tables.

White Ash Mine Park is a great site for young bike riders and those just starting out, with gentle gradients, smooth surfaces and different loop options. The playground is surrounded by a paved circular path, which then links into a 0.25 mile paved fitness trail contouring the park's edge. At the north end of the park there are 2 smooth surfaced basketball courts at opposing angles. The colored marker lines make great fun for cycling games or running around. The south and east sides of this park are maintained as tall grass wildlife areas and play a role in water drainage. The fringes of this grassland support many wildflowers and insects. In the fall the paths can be littered with slow-moving grasshoppers trying to warm up in the sunshine. Bring a bug-collecting box to look at them close up.

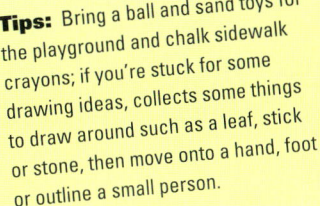

Tips: Bring a ball and sand toys for the playground and chalk sidewalk crayons; if you're stuck for some drawing ideas, collects some things to draw around such as a leaf, stick or stone, then move onto a hand, foot or outline a small person.

Bring chalk for some drawing fun

Other options:

1. Biking Loop. Bike trail link to City of Golden loop trail and playground at New Loveland Mine Park. Distance: 0.4 miles. From White Ash Drive turn left into Iowa Street. Follow the sidewalk on the south side of the road until just before the traffic lights on Hwy93. Take the right fork southwards through Magpie Gulch, a landscaped open space corridor, to the footbridge across Hwy93. Turn right after onto Rubey Drive—you are now opposite Mitchell Elementary School. Follow the wide pavement south to link with New Loveland Mine Park and the City multiuse trail bike loop at 5th street (pg 143).

2. Mitchell Elementary School. 2 playgrounds and lots of paved sidewalks and parking for honing bike-riding skills when school is not in session.

• •

You could also theme a trip by looking at the different types of seed heads in the grasses and flowers bordering the path. See the difference between those that blow away versus 'sticky' ones that catch on clothes.

Recent dumping and mounding of soil at the north end of White Ash Mine Park (summer 2006) has made this part of the park more sheltered. Landscaping is scheduled for late 2006.

25 WHITE RANCH PARK

Almost too good to be true. Scramble on and around old farm machinery to your heart's content along a 0.2 mile self-guided trail on a former homestead site. Learn how they made hay in the old days, then picnic either in open grassland or under the shade of large pine trees and enjoy cool breezes with views in all directions.

White Ranch Park

Belcher Hill, Golden, CO 80403
Jefferson County Open Space
303 271 5925
www.jeffco.us/openspace/openspace

Location: 10.8 miles from Golden Visitor Center.

Directions: Go north on Washington Avenue for 1 mile. Turn right on Hwy93. Turn left at the stoplight onto Golden Gate Canyon Road and follow this for 3.8 miles. Turn right onto Crawford Gulch Road. Follow this for about 4 miles until White Ranch Park is signed on the right. Turn right onto Belcher Hill and drive to its end. Follow the unpaved road until it ends at the parking lot.

Parking: Gravel parking lot with space for 40 vehicles.

Season: Spring, summer and fall. At 7,500 feet, the Farm Machinery Trail is exposed. Avoid midday heat and windy days. There is good shade from large pine trees at the end of the trail. Bring extra clothing in case of sudden weather changes.

Restrooms: Two vault restrooms located about 0.2 miles from the parking lot.

Water: No.

Dogs: Yes. On-leash.

White Ranch Park is one of Jefferson County's largest Open Space properties and encompasses open meadows, forested foothills, a pristine canyon, buttes and rock formations. The park is named after Paul R. White whose family operated a Hereford cattle ranch from 1913-1969. Although driving to White Ranch Park requires something of a circuitous route, it's worth it to spend some time in a beautiful foothills location far away from any road traffic.

The most significant feature which will captivate the under 5's, and any history-minded adult, is the display of old farming machinery dating from the 1880's. All were pulled by a two horse team and used to prepare the ground for crops whether it was breaking ground, harrowing, drilling seed, spreading manure or cutting and gathering hay. The machinery is laid out to the east of the parking lot over an easy gradient trail for 0.2 miles, stroller and wheelchair accessible. There are small signs at each piece of machinery describing how it was used. You can even see a 19th century horse drawn version of a muck spreader with a floor that moves like a conveyor belt—all rather ingenious. No child will be able to resist sitting on the old metal seats, although these 100 year old items should be treated with care. Look for wildflowers as you pass through open meadow. The trail ends in an extended picnic area

POUY KENDAL ATCHISON-BOTH

Tips: Look for the blue flash and undulating flight of the Mountain Bluebird, a summer visitor to Colorado. Don't forget your camera for pictures of grinning kids on top of old farm machines. If you want quiet, visit mid-week; you might not see a soul.

Other options:

1. Back Country Camping. If you fancy a FREE back country camping experience with your kids, White Ranch offers two options both under 1.5 miles from this parking lot. Campsites are equipped with running water, stacked wood supply, restrooms, food storage lockers and picnic tables. Read the information on site, pick up a brochure, or call 303 271 5948 www.co.jefferson.co.us/openspace/openspace

2. Mount Galbraith Park 6,300 feet. This trailhead canyon location gives a wilder feel close to town. Although better known for its steep and rocky trails, a quiet midweek visit provides opportunities to explore in the vicinity of the trailhead in the sometimes dry/sometimes wet Tucker Gulch. Exposed rock, a range of vegetation and large cottonwoods give the place a secluded feel. If you just make it up the first two zigzags you get views from a rocky point. Great for fall color around the Gulch. Directions: From Hwy93 take Golden Gate Canyon Road west for about 1.5 miles. The park entrance is signed on the left, (south) side of the road. See http://jeffco.us/openspace/openspace

• •

under large pine trees, where there are also restrooms. At its far end near Longhorn Trail, a large shelter can be used if you get caught in a downpour.

Back at the parking lot, the large perimeter boulders glitter with flakes of mica. Point these out to your kids or simply let them climb the rocks.

OTHER LOCATIONS

Clear Creek Canyon
Hwy6 and I70 corridor
from Golden to Loveland Pass.

Beat the heat or just passing through .....

Clear Creek Canyon/Hwy6

There are many opportunities to pull off the road and get down to the rushing waters of Clear Creek, but in many cases the sites are right next to the road or the access to Clear Creek is steep.

Carlson Elementary Playground

Tunnel 1 Trail—5,807 feet

For the adventurous we recommend a stop at Tunnel 1, 1 mile west up Hwy6 from the junction with Hwy93. This location leaves the road and sound of cars behind on a quiet half-mile (one way) walk around a large bend in the canyon. This is one of the few places where you can imagine what the canyon was like before the highway was engineered. Pull in carefully to a gravel shoulder on the left side of the tunnel (look for the sign saying 'Tunnel 1' on the arch). There's usually space for about 8 vehicles. Descend a short steep slope towards the river for 50 yards—small children and strollers may need to be carried. There is a popular summer swimming hole here (beware strong currents). From here it's an easy walk on level ground around the cliff base with numerous points to get close to the creek. Beware high flow rate during spring runoff. Kids like the changing scenery as you keep going round the bend towards the highway. Retrace your steps as the bend nears the highway. Note: There are no restrooms on this stretch of the corridor.

Idaho Springs

7,524 feet. I70 Exits 241 and 242

There's plenty to do in Idaho Springs but we've singled out the following to distract the under 5's:

Carlson Elementary School, located on Canyon Boulevard and 14th Avenue, has a large and very unusual wooden playground structure over 80 feet long. More gothic than modern, this playground consists of linked wooden pathways, castle-like towers, swing bridges, lookouts, tire climbs and a wooden stage. The potential for hide and seek is endless. There is also a separate, though less intriguing, tots area. Look for changes at this site with community efforts underway to upgrade landing surfaces and reduce splinter potential. Use this area when school is not in session. Wear old clothes—the tires leave marks, and avoid hot windless days when the courtyard location can bake.

Other Idaho Springs attractions include **Engine No 60 and railway carriage** located at the south end of 17th Street. This narrow gauge train was typical of the locomotives used in the mountain towns. Climb on board the engine and walk alongside its length on a raised wooden platform.

Visit the **Courtney Ryley Cooper Parks** next to Clear Creek at Canyon Boulevard and 24th, opposite Idaho Springs Visitor Center. This linear, shaded grass picnic area gives great access to the creek and has a small older style playground with swings at its east end. Cross over 24th to the west side of Clear Creek to enjoy the park away from the main road. The Visitor Center also has a free museum which may be of interest to the under 5s.

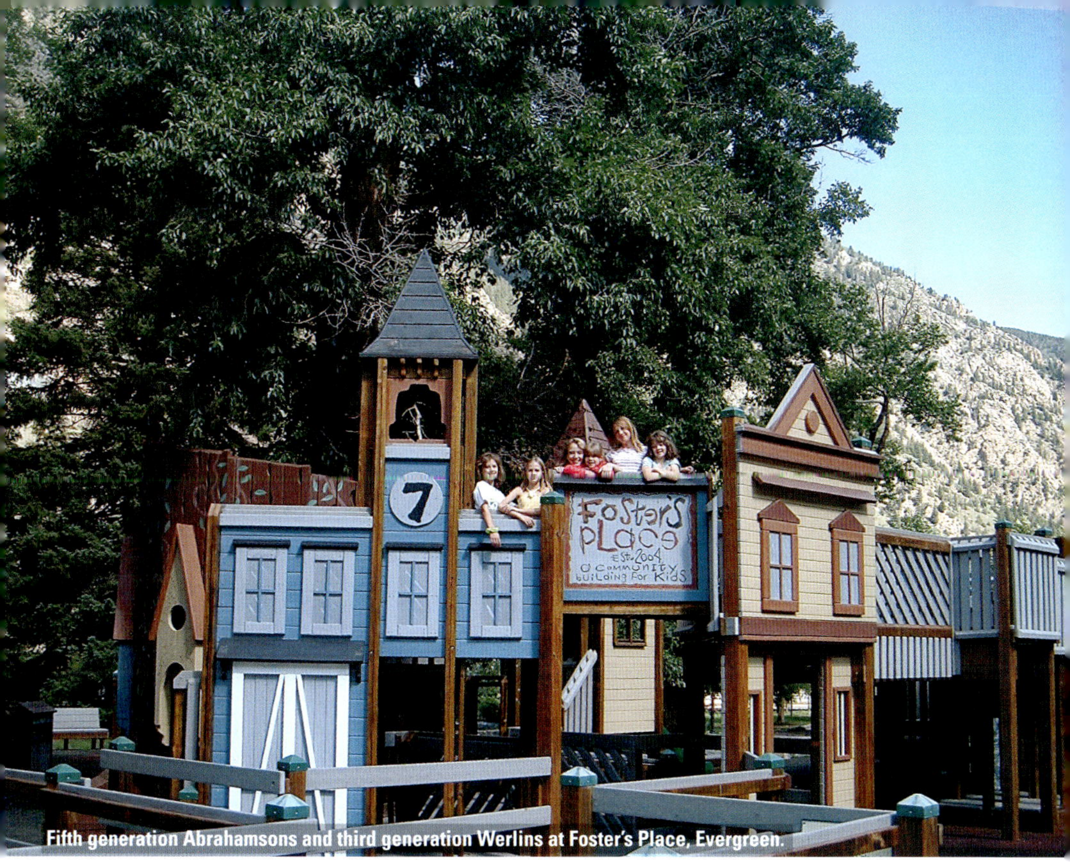

Fifth generation Abrahamsons and third generation Werlins at Foster's Place, Evergreen.

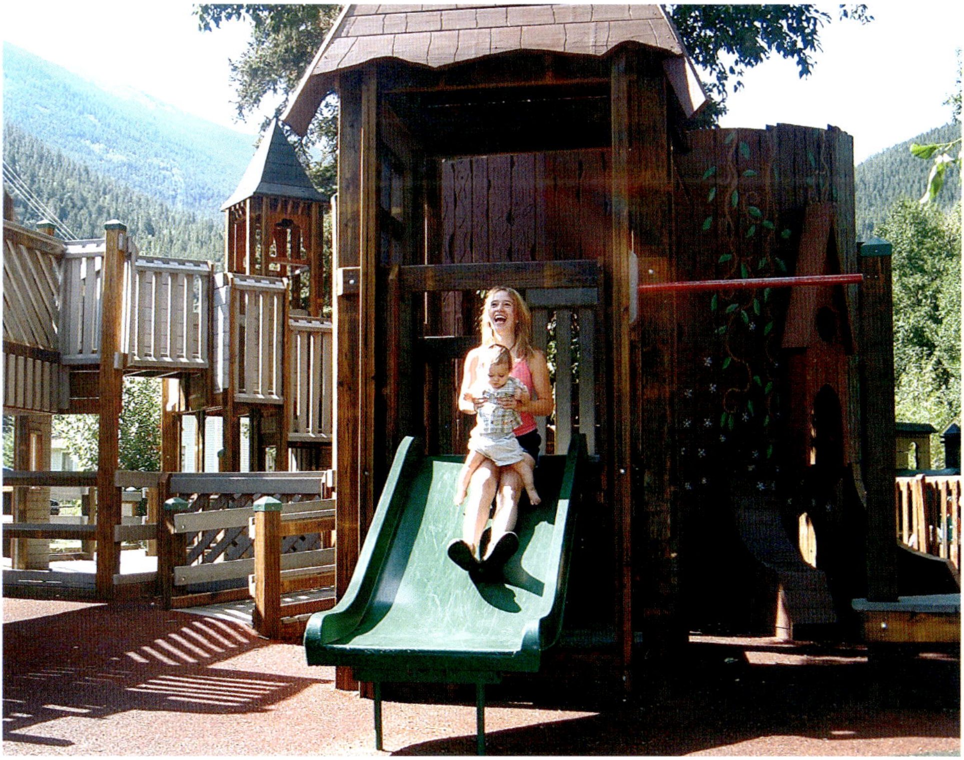

DANA ABRAHAMSON, HISTORIC EVERGREEN, INC. - ALL

Georgetown

8,512 feet. I70 Exit 228

Forget the train, the best attraction for kids in Georgetown is **Foster's Place at City Park;** one of the most fun, unusual and creative playgrounds in Clear Creek Mountain country not to mention

juvenile mountain sheep

the Colorado Front Range. Inspired by a brave little boy called Foster who loved trains, the resulting 2004 playground is exemplary in showing what can be achieved through community effort and partnership. A castle like-structure winds around an old cottonwood tree with ramps, swing bridges and passages linking different areas. There is a hidden tire swing, puppet stage, wooden train and sandbox and that's only half the features. City Park is located at 10th Street and Taos Street. Families visit here from Denver and word is spreading. See for yourself.

Other attractions: Look for Rocky Mountain Bighorn Sheep from the Wildlife Viewing Station at the north end of Georgetown Lake. Fish in Georgetown Lake for 3 different types of trout—under 16's do not require a license.

Silver Plume

9,118 feet. I70 Exit 226

A small town of around 200 with a name inspired, some say, by a vein of silver so rich that silver flakes broke off in feather-like patterns. Stop at Silver Plume to explore this Victorian mining town and another community inspired playground. **Dinger's Park** (named after the abandoned placer claim originally worked by Dinger Williams) is located next to Clear Creek and opposite George Row Museum at the west end of Main Street. The Park contains new playground equipment after a year long community fund-raising effort.

Loveland Pass

11,990 feet. I70 Exit 216. Follow Hwy6 to reach Loveland Pass summit.

There are two options:

1. **Divide Trail.** Park at the summit and follow a steadily climbing ridge trail on the west side of the road that eventually takes you onto the Continental Divide at 12,585 feet. Enjoy the views and alpine flowers, and jump in snow patches until at least late June early July. Don't be surprised (although certainly don't promise!) if you come across a shaggy herd of mountain goats seeking the cool breezes. Avoid windy days and be aware of thunderstorms from midday onwards.

2. **Pass Lake 11,835 feet.**

For a more mellow and level environment, continue over Loveland Pass summit, descend for about two miles, and look for a right turn and large paved parking lot. This location has one large lake—Pass Lake—and two smaller connecting lakes set amid scree slopes and wildflower meadows. Large stands of bushes provide shelter on windy days and gravel/sandy tracks provide easy access between the lakes. Consider bringing a bike along for your more able biker while you walk around. This is a beautiful spot.

For both the Loveland Pass sites bring, and drink, plenty of water to avoid altitude headaches.

Foster's Place

Divide Trail, Loveland Pass

INDEX

Anderson Park 149
Andrew's Arboretum 33
Ann U. White Trail 24
Arapahoe Ridge Park. 96
Artesian Springs Resort, Eldorado 55
Arvada Blunn Reservoir 96
Barber Park playground.. 86
Bass Lake 149
Bear Canyon Trail - unpaved 80
Bear Creek. 80
Bear Creek Greenbelt.. 101
Bear Creek Greenway 76
Bear Creek Lake Park 99
Bear Creek Reservoir 100
Bear Creek Trail – paved multiuse 77
Beverly Heights Park. 102
Big Soda Lake 99
Birds Nest Disc Golf Park, Arvada 97
Bobolink Trail 50
Bohn Park 73
Boulder Canyon - History Trail 54
Boulder County Recycling Center 28
Boulder Creek 30
Boulder Creek Trail 33
Boulder Dushanbe Teahouse 30
Boulder Farmer's Market 30
Boulder Map Gallery 33
Boulder Museum of Contemporary Art (BMoCA) . . 31
Boulder Public Library 31
Boulder Rock Club, climbing boulder 64
Broadway Community Plaza 83
Broadway Trail – paved multiuse 77
Buffalo Bill Museum, Grave, Overlook and cafe 138
Carlson Elementary School Playground. 160
Cambrian Lime Kiln 103
Castle Rock, South Table Mountain 104
Charles A. Haertling Sculpture Garden 32
Chautauqua Park 34
Children's Peace Garden 65
Church Ditch. 151
City Park, Boulder. 89
Clear Creek Canyon, Tunnel 1 Trail 161
Clear Creek History Park 108
Clear Creek Trail - multiuse. 144
Clear Creek Trail Sculpture Loop 106
Clear Creek White Water Park 132
Colorado Railroad Museum.. 109
Colorado School of Mines campus 111
Colorado School of Mines Geology Museum. 111
Colorado School of Mines Geology Trail 111
Community Ditch Trail 74
Continental Divide Trail.. 162
Coot Lake 38
Cottonwood Marsh and Boardwalk 90
Courtney Ryley Cooper Parks and Playground 160

Creekside Elementary School playgrounds 77
Crown Hill Lake 113
Crown Hill Park 113
Crown Rock, Flagstaff Mountain 42
CU Natural History Museum and Campus 46
Dakota Ridge Trail 118
Davidson Ditch Trail 74
Dinger's Park 162
Dinosaur Ridge 115
Discovery Park. 155
Doudy Draw Trailhead 58
Dude's Fishing Hole 123
East Boulder Community Center 49
East Boulder Dog Park 49
East Mapleton Avenue playground 62
Eaton Park BMX bike track 41
Eaton Park Nature Trail 41
Eben G. Fine Park 52
Eisenhower Elementary School playgrounds 26
Eldorado - Artesian Springs Resort 55
Eldorado Canyon State Park. 55
Elephant Rock 54
Enchanted Mesa Trail 37
Engine No 60 and railway carriage 160
Engineering Building 48
Estates Park 131
Evert Pierson Kid's Fishing Ponds 32
Fairmount Park 119
Fairmount Trail 151
Fire Crusher Trail 151
Fiske Planetarium and Science Center 48
Flagstaff Mountain 42
Flagstaff Mountain Nature Center 45
Foothills Community Park 59
Foothills Dog Park 60
Fossil Trace Club House 155
Foster's Place, City Park 162
Fourmile Creek Trailhead 25
Georgetown Lake 162
Glacier Ice Cream.. 64
Golden City Bike Loop Trail 143
Golden Cliffs Preserve 121
Golden Community Center 132
Golden Farmer's Market 107
Golden Gate Canyon State Park 126
Golden Heights Park 131
Golden Public Library – Jefferson County 108
Goose Creek Greenway 62
Goose Creek Trail Loop 64
Gregory Canyon – Amphitheatre Trail 45
Harlow Platts Park 69
Harlow Platts Park Disc Golf Course 70
Hawthorn Community Gardens 65
Haystack Mountain Goat Dairy 41
Heritage Dells Park 103

Holiday Park, Yarmouth Avenue... 61
Homemade Park... 144
Idaho Springs... 160
Jefferson County Fairgrounds... 129
Johnson Park, Wheat Ridge... 149
Kestrel Pond Urban Wildlife Sanctuary... 113
Kinney Run Trail... 103
Lions Park and Kayak Park... 132
Long's Iris Gardens... 67
Lookout Mountain Nature Center and Preserve... 136
Lookout Mountain Road... 102
Loveland Pass... 162
Lubahn Trailhead, Castle Rock... 104
Lyons Sculpture Trail... 72
Lyons Soda Fountain... 73
Lyons, Town of... 71
Magpie Gulch Trail... 145
Marshall Mesa... 74
Martin Park... 76
Matt's Whitewater Park... 52
Maxwell Lake and Park... 94
McClintock Trail... 37
Meadow Park, Lyons... 71
Mesa Trail, South Trailhead... 58
Mitchell Elementary School playgrounds... 145
Morrison Ridge, bouldering... 100
Morrison, town of... 118
Mount Galbraith Park, trailhead... 159
Mount Sanitas Trailheads and Bouldering... 83
NCAR... 78
New Loveland Mine Park... 144
Norlin Quadrangle... 48
Norman D. Memorial Park... 141
North Boulder Park... 81
North Boulder Recreation Center... 65
North Boulder Reservoir – bike loop... 41
North Golden Bike Loop... 143
North Table Mountain Quarry... 139
North Table Mountain – Golden Cliffs Preserve... 121
North Teller Trailhead... 29
NREL... 146
Panorama Point... 123
Paramount Park... 114
Parfet Historic Reserve... 152
Parfet Park... 106
Pass Lake... 162
Pearl Street Mall... 84
Prairie Dog Interpretative Trail... 40
Prospect Lake, Arvada... 148
Prospect Park... 148
Raccoon Trail... 124
Ralston Creek Trail... 126
Ranch Ponds... 126
Red Rocks – Settlers Park... 89
Red Rocks Park... 118
Reverend's Ridge Campground... 128
Rock Park – Arapahoe Ridge Park... 26
Saint Vrain Creek... 71
Sawhill Ponds Wildlife Preserve... 92
Scott Carpenter Outdoor Pool... 88

Scott Carpenter Park... 87
Scott Carpenter Skate and Bike Park... 88
Settlers Park... 89
Shakespeare Garden... 48
Shining Mountain Waldorf School playground... 61
Silverplume, Dinger's Park... 162
Snowshoe Hare Trail... 125
South Boulder Creek... 49
South Boulder Creek Trail... 75
South Boulder Recreation Center... 70
South Table Mountain – North end... 104
South Table Mountain – South end... 146,147
South Teller Trailhead... 29
Streamside Trail... 56
Supremacy Slabs... 57
Table Mesa Shopping Center... 77
Tanglewood Sports Park and playground... 147
Tantra Park... 70
Teller Farm Trail... 29
Terry Grant Park... 132
Tom Watson City Park... 38
Tony Grampsas Dog Park... 151
Tony Grampsas Memorial Sports Complex... 150
Triceratops Trail... 152
Tucker Gulch Trail – multiuse... 142
Twin Lakes... 41
University Hill Elementary School playground... 48
Vanover Park... 144
Viele Lake... 69
Walden Ponds Wildlife Habitat... 91
Walter Orr Roberts Weather Trail... 78
Welch Ditch... 103
West Arvada Dog Park... 97
Westernaires Training Arena... 131
Wheat Ridge Greenbelt Corridor... 148
White Ash Mine Park... 156
White Ranch Park... 158
White Rocks Trail... 92
Wilbur and Nellie Larkin Pond Trail... 126
Wildlife Viewing Station Rocky Mountain Bighorn... 162
Wonderland Lake... 93

Further Reading and References

Bell, Trudy E. Bicycling with children - A Complete How-To Guide. The Mountaineers, 1999
Blakey, Nancy. Go outside: Over 130 activities for Outdoor Adventures. Tricycle Press, 2002
Carlson, Laurie and Judith Dammel. Kids Camp! Chicago Review Press, 1995.
Chiras, Dan. Eco Kids: Raising Children Who Care for the Earth. New Society Pulishers, 2005.
Collison, Linda and Russell, Bob. Colorado Kids. Pruett Publishing Company, 1997.
Cornell, Joseph. Sharing Nature with Children. Dawn Publications, 1998.
Downham, Topher, Steven J. Mertz, and Dinah S. Pollard. Boulder Area Accessible Trails and Natural Sites. CTRS, 2000. Boulder Parks and Recreation EXPAND Program, CTRS, 2000. Http://www.ci.bouldewr.us/openspace/publications.htm
Drewes, Harald and John Townrow. Trailwalker's Guide to the Dinosuar Ridge, Red Rocks and Green Mountain area. Friends of Dinosaur Ridge, Morrison, CO, 2005.
Ellison, Sheila and Judith Gray. 365 Days of Creative Play: For children 2 years and up. Sourcebooks Inc, 1995.
Ferranti, Philip. Colorado State Parks: a complete recreation guide. The Mountaineers, 1996.
Green, Stewart M. Rock Climbing Colorado. Falcon Press Publishing, 1995.
Hanket, Glen. Boulder Urban Trails: "Take a Bike" series. C.A.K. publishing, 2004.
Hanket, Glen. Jefferson County Central Urban Trails: "Take a Bike" series. C.A.K. publishing, 2004.
Hirschfield, Cindy. Canine Colorado. Fulcrum Publishing, 2001
Hubbel, Pete. Classic Rock Climbs Golden Cliffs, Colorado. Chockstone Press, Inc. 1997
Joyce, Gary. Climbing with Children. 1996 Menasha Ridge Press, 1996.
Keilty, Maureen. Best Hikes with Children - Colorado. The Mountaineers, 2005.
Kennedy, Doris. Fun with the family. Colorado. Globe Pequot Press, 2005.

Lingelbach, Jenepher. Hands-On Nature: Information and Activities for Exploring the Environment With Children. University Press of New England, 2000.

Louv, Richard. Last Child in the Woods: Saving Our Children from Nature-Deficit Disorder. Algonquin Books of Chapel Hill, 2005

Norman, Cathleen. Golden Old and New - a walking tour guide. Colorado Mountain Club, 1996.

Northwest Earth Institute. Discovering a Sense of Place: Discussion Course on. Northwest Earth Institute, 2000.

Potter, Jean. Nature in a Nutshell for kids: Over 100 activities you can do in 10 minutes or less. Jon Wiley and Sons, Inc., 1995.

Sobel, David. Mapmaking with Children: Sense of Place Education for the Elementary Years. Heinemann, 1998.

WEBSITES

http://gorp.away.com/gorp/publishers/pruett/den_kids.htm
activities and outings with kids
Mother's and More—Stroller Walks in Boulder County
http://www.dodemonster.com/bcmm/stroller.html

ABOUT THE AUTHOR

Kath Pyke lives with her husband and two small children in Golden, Colorado. Formerly from the UK, she has spent the last 10 years living in Boulder and Golden. Something of an adventurer, she has climbed new routes around the world; ranging from remote islands off Scotland and steep granite walls in Madagascar to long alpine routes in the Colorado Rockies. With degrees in both Biology and Resource Management, she has worked for the past 20 years in conservation and land management where projects have ranged from planting 'heirloom orchards' in school grounds to searching for the giant flying squirrel in Pakistan. She is a strong advocate for taking some daily risk and getting intimate with your local park, stream or ditch.